JUST ME,

Insights From
a Reluctant Medium

by

Justin Pearce

authorHOUSE®

AuthorHouse™ UK Ltd.
500 Avebury Boulevard
Central Milton Keynes, MK9 2BE
www.authorhouse.co.uk
Phone: 08001974150

First published by AuthorHouse 6/10/2008

ISBN: 978-1-4343-7938-2 (sc)

Printed in the United States of America
Bloomington, Indiana

This book is printed on acid-free paper.

INTRODUCTION

MY NAME IS Justin and I am a psychic medium.

This means that I have the ability to connect people with the spirits of those that have passed away before us.

I believe you have chosen this book for a reason. Please keep an open mind while you discover what this book has to offer you.

This book has been split into four separate parts. It starts with my life. It follows with a section that covers ways of accessing your own ability. Then there are extracts from my work as a medium. It finishes with various questions and answers.

It is designed to be a kind of manual for anyone that may have feelings or abilities they are unsure about and questions they just don't know where to go with.

This is by no means my life story, but what I have written about myself, will hopefully, give you an insight into the things that go on in the world of an ordinary man, with an ability that has helped many. You may be able to identify with what I have been through in your own life, trying to come to terms living everyday with the world of spirit. It maybe of interest to anyone that has even the mildest curiosity in what a medium does and how the process of spirit connection works. More importantly, it will show that anyone can learn to live with the world of spirit, everyday.

My life has certainly been a strange one. It's been full of ups and downs with denials about what I have and what I am capable of doing.

This is my guide for you. It has been co-written by my best friend Mark. If it wasn't for him, this book would be a rambling mess with no style or finesse whatsoever. Harder to read than War and Peace in Icelandic!

I trust that whatever you find will be useful and at the very least - interesting.

Thank you.
Justin
JANUARY 2008

Contents

SECTION THREE: *Connections*

SECTION FOUR *Questions and Answers*

SECTION ONE:
My Life

Chapter One

JUST A DISTANT HUM

Narberth, West Wales
September 1970

81 HOURS.

That's how long my mum was in labour for.

My parents were both living with my Grandmother at the time. Nerves were a little frail - they all found it very difficult to live together. Both were from small close-knit towns and had met, fallen in love and got married after a year or so. My mum was only 19 years old when she went into labour .My dad - a chef in the Royal Navy - was due to be a father at the tender age of 21. He paced up and down the ward. He was full of nerves. Not just in the way that a husband would be in this situation, but deeper concerns were there too.

My dad always found that whenever a good thing in his life came along it was usually followed by something terrible. As it turned out, his fears were warranted - today was to be no exception to the rule.

Still pacing and wondering when I was going to make my grand entrance. He started to get more and more annoyed with the lack of information. He was shouting at the doctors but no-one was telling him anything. He wanted to know why it was taking so long and, quite understandably, why my mum had been left in the geriatric ward and not on the maternity ward where she should be.

A few hours later my Uncle Richard turned up. A well known, well respected man of quite a forbidding size and attitude. He asked the same questions as my dad, only a lot louder and to the right people. They eventually started to get the information they sought, although my father's nerves were still in tatters as he continued to pace up and down the corridor.

An hour or so later at 8.45am I was dragged by forceps kicking and screaming into the open air. The Doctors checked me over and asked the Nurse to sort out the necessary. The Nurse went about her business as normal but stopped in her tracks, turning to the Doctor.

There was another baby.

They hadn't realized at all that my mum was having twins. Ultrasound was something that was not really available at that time and it was easy to miss something of such importance. After a lot of shouting and running around they delivered my brother Jason into the world.

He had died.

They buried him a few days later in a small white coffin in the Tabernacle Church in Narberth, Pembrokeshire. In a grave with no markings. I meanwhile, slept in an incubator with a small teddy bear that was far bigger than me. They said to my parents that Jason had died due to lack of oxygen.

It's only now that I realize that I was given the chance of life for a reason when we both came into the world. I was meant to stay here and work while Jason stayed on the other side in the world of spirit to guide me through what has become a rollercoaster of a life.

I still don't fully understand my connection to a world that is both feared and denied. I know I am here to help people get an understanding of what happens when they lose someone close and a stronger understanding of their own spirituality.

Chapter Two

THINGS THAT GO BUMP IN THE NIGHT.

*Portsmouth,
November 1980*

THE CORNER OF my bedroom where the spooky ghosts lived was very dark at night.

Of course, they all existed in the mind of a 10 year old boy, but to me they were real. I could almost hear them whispering in the dark, preparing to pounce and scare the crap out of me as all ghosts did.

Luckily enough I had a secret weapon. The best ghost repellent money could buy and better than any thermo-nuclear device, a small bedside light.

If I kept that switched on it would keep them at bay – I knew this to be true. The problem was I still knew they were there and I wasn't about to fall asleep so they could get me.

So, each night after mum and dad were convinced I had gone to bed, the bedside light would come on, my bulky headphones would come out and I would listen to the radio, I was hoping it wasn't going to be heard by my parents, who would've undoubtedly removed my stereo, which for a ten year old boy would be worse than any ghostly ambush.

Eventually, with the bedside light and the radio repelling the ghosts, I had begun to relax a little, lost in the happy melodies swirling in my ears.

Then the moment came that changed everything for me.

At first I caught a glimpse out of the corner of a sleepy eye and then lazily I focused on the new addition to my room.

Someone was standing at the end of the bed.

I thought maybe I was dreaming but it seemed more likely to be one of my dad's old navy friends judging from the blue military uniform he wore.

He was just looking at me,
Smiling pleasantly.

I was by now wide awake and removed my headphones and turned off my radio, scared that I had been caught by my dad's friend. He would surely tell my parents how naughty I was.

Strangely enough, I wasn't really scared of this man that I had never seen before. I was, of course, taught never ever to talk to strangers. But this was somehow different. It was in my room and whatever I felt was definitely not hostile intention – not like the spooky ghosts plotting in the corner.

I don't remember how late it was but the rest of the house was quiet. Not even the faint sounds of the TV downstairs or my parents talking.

Before I could say anything he introduced himself.

"Hello, I'm James, James Saunders…" He said in calming, agreeable tones.

"…You must be Justin?"

I nodded then asked politely what he wanted, assuming all the while he was there to tell me off for staying up.

"I have come to see you Justin" He continued.

"I am here to tell you something, you are here to help"

I had a million questions.

What?

Help with what?

Are you going to tell my dad I'm up?

Yet before I could ask, he was gone.
Just like that.
I blinked and he had vanished.

Now, I would like to say that as the psychic medium I am now, I was calm, collected and understood exactly what had happened.

As it turned out, I screamed like a big girl and ran into my mum and dads room rambling incoherently about the navy ghost man in my room. They had obviously had a lot of experience with my midnight ranting, and, as usual, took me back to my room to show me that there were no ghosts in my room, the walls weren't wobbling and the monsters weren't lurking under the bed.

I don't think I slept at all that night. For that matter, I don't think I slept for a quite a few nights after that.

Little did I realise that this was the first of many encounters with spirit, which would lead to a life of many ups and downs and inner questions about what I do. It was the start of a new path that would lead to meeting some of the most amazing people and more importantly – being of help to others in ways I could never have dreamed...

I just didn't know it yet.

Chapter Three

END OF THE BEGINNING

FROM THE AGE of ten, after my late night meeting with James Saunders, things had changed. I ended up a few years later with my parents in a military memorabilia shop in the centre of Portsmouth. It was there that I stumbled upon the uniform that my late night guest had been wearing when I saw him.... I discovered it was a Royal Air Force uniform and not from the Royal Navy as I had assumed.

At around 13 years old I found a thirst for knowledge had been created and I wanted to know more about what had happened.

I checked with the library for any information and they were extremely helpful. I managed to discover that James Saunders had indeed been an RAF pilot and had been shot down during the later years of World War 2. He was 27

That was all I needed.

Now I was really cooking with gas.

I had developed a fascination with ghost stories and the supernatural in general. My mum told me all about my Grandmother (Her Mother) being a psychic. I just thought it was that she could tell the future. At that age I wasn't really aware of what the metaphysical and supernatural world had to offer. Up until a few years before I didn't know it was possible to talk to the dead. Ghosts were ghosts. Monsters were monsters. Some people could tell the future. That was about all I knew until then.

It also transpired that my father's dad was also very gifted within the world of spirit.

So, I was hooked. My Mother would come home from a bookshop in town with a spooky storybook almost every week. At school all my projects were based around haunted houses, psychics, graveyards, vampires and werewolves. - I also knew that the area we lived in was a hotspot for haunting. It was (and still is) called Gatcombe Park. The site, before it became a housing estate, used to be an Army barracks. To this very day is still referred to by many as Hilsea Barracks. A high brick wall still surrounds the housing estate that would have been the perimeter around the Army camp. I decided to do some research for a piece of work I was doing with a friend at school on ghost stories from the local area. We went down to the Library again (real regulars by now), and got into the records office. The lady behind the counter checked us out and made sure that we weren't going to touch anything that we shouldn't. After a thorough interrogation, but, alas no strip search, she gave us some powdered gloves and allowed us to view plans and maps of the area – some from around 1600 a.d. (which was pretty much a castle, two huts, three wenches and two pigs)!. It turned out that Gatcombe House, which was centered in the barracks and had always given me the creeps, was an old memorial hospital. I was also told that there was a graveyard that spread out over the whole estate before the barracks was built. So I decided to ask the local people whether or not they had experienced anything like a haunting.

Did they have wobbly walls or ghosts in one corner of the room?

It turned out that a house down the street had been haunted for a long time and its current occupants had decided to get their house exorcised by a priest. Things were apparently flying off the walls at them, laughter was heard from empty bedrooms and belongings were moved. The owners would try experiments when it first started occurring, they would put something, like an item of jewelry, on the floor and walk out of the room. When they came back into the room the jewelery would be moved and they couldn't find it, no matter how hard they looked. It would turn up a few houses away in a friend's laundry basket.

Go figure!

Things were also happening in our house.

My mum was lying in the garden lapping up the sun one summer, eyes closed, relaxing in the heat, when she suddenly felt the whole weight of a person lie on top of her. She thought it was my dad messing around, she opened her eyes with a start, but there was no one there despite the pressing sensation. She shouted out as loud as she could and whatever was there suddenly ceased.

It didn't end there. One day my dad was fitting some shelves in my sister's room when my mum called him. He was about to leave when suddenly the bedroom door slammed shut in his face. There was no wind in the bedroom and also there were thick pile carpets in the room. You had to use some considerable force to close the door any other time.

This all went on for quite some time.

Mum had tried using Ouija boards in the house to try and contact whoever was making the noises at night and bothering us. She had at first found them fascinating and amazing. But after a while it spooked her a little. Some of the information she was receiving were of a threatening type so she stopped using them. I still don't agree with the use of these boards in any circumstance, as they are very dangerous. These are an open door to the other side, for negative energies that may, (for whatever reason), want to cause trouble. It's like leaving your front door open during the day and hoping to get your house cleaned by whoever comes in. More than likely you will be cleaned out!

As far as my own personal experiences were concerned, after the James Saunders incident, very little happened – kind of. I used to get weird feelings whenever I would come into contact with certain people. It was like a vibe. I would know things about them – little things…. like small details that I had no way of knowing…. A person's name or what they did for a living. Sometimes I would have an idea where they lived or who they were related to. Just minor detail but quite accurate more often than not. I was still far too sensitive all the time. Very touchy and emotional. I knew my period hadn't started. For one thing I was male. And I was far too young to be going through the male menopause! Things would drive me nuts. If someone was horrible to me it would play on my mind for days. Arguments would have me wrestling with self-doubt and loathing for even longer. I hoped it was just a part of growing up.

Strangely, after a few years of visitations, ghostly sightings and noises, things just seemed to go away of their own accord – personally and around me. I don't know what happened, but over a period of time the activities just sort of filtered out. Maybe I just didn't notice so much - my rebellious years took over and my interests were more of loud music, motorbikes, action films and girls.

Especially girls!

When I look back, it's a shame really. After my initial visit from Mr. Saunders, I wasn't scared or nervous of such encounters and I had literally been de-sensitized by the daily occurrences.

I didn't even need my bedside light any more.

So, I was becoming to all intents and purposes, a "normal" young tearaway. I went out with my friends, smoked cigarettes, did rude things with girls, drank beer and caused far too much trouble as all bad guys do.

The only other thing that happened was when I was about 18.

I had a friend called Mark who lived on the estate.

For a longtime we were inseparable. We would hangout together all summer. Going to Hilsea Lido swimming pool and meeting with girls. We would take our ghetto blaster tape recorder with us and listen to the Human League, Depeche Mode, and Howard Jones - Whoever was popular at the time. Mark was a year older than me but because of my birthday being in September he was two school years ahead of me.

We would meet up outside our school, City of Portsmouth Boys after 3 o'clock, and run over to chat with the girls at Mayfield School – our arch enemies (the boys that is!). Our summers were spent riding our bikes to Horndean, just outside Portsmouth, to see Debbie and Ivy, a couple of lovely girls we were very close to. Debbie had a house out in the country and we would spend summers lying in the nearby fields, talking and having fun.

They were great days and I have some amazing memories of that time. A few years later, Mark had moved to a town called Fareham and had a new circle of friends. We were both working at that time but still kept in contact every now and again.

Mark was cycling to work on 1st April 1989. He was hit by a drunk driver and killed. He was just 20 years old.

I hadn't felt right all that night or day. It was my mum's birthday but I still felt something was wrong. Something I couldn't explain. I went out and bought a paper. Before I picked it up, I saw the headline. It said that a lot of people had been killed on the roads that night. The feeling swept over me that someone I knew would be amongst the names.

Sure enough it was Mark.

I double checked it and checked again.

Our mutual friend, Bob, came over to the house and confirmed it. We just couldn't believe it had happened.

Mark had gone. And somehow I had known.

Why was my friend gone?

Would I ever see him again?

Nothing else remotely spiritual would occur for another few years.

Chapter Four

SMALL ACORNS AND MIGHTY OAKS

I MET MY first wife, Sarah, through a blind date.

A work colleague introduced us after I had told him that I was reluctantly very single and, well....kind of looking. His partner at the time had a friend in the same boat. Inevitably, and rather sneakily, they decided to set us up on a date.

I liked her immediately.

We had a lot in common and I really felt a strong attraction. It wasn't very long before we were smitten. So much so, we bought a house together almost a year later.

During one deep conversation about life, the universe and everything, Sarah informed me that— and I suppose in the great scheme of things this comes as no surprise - she was a psychic medium.

"A what?" I said with some bewilderment.

Her response didn't help one iota.

"I can talk with dead people"

Now, at 23 years old, I had had very little to do with my psychic past. The metaphysical thread that ran through my family was not as important as paying the bills, buying records and going for a beer with my friends. In fact, very little "phenomena" had happened in 10 years. Even the visit from James Saunders was a distant memory.

Damn! I was a Shipping Agent. I didn't go in for that mumbo jumbo voodoo stuff and told her so.

During one conversation she had said that I was about as psychic as a wet flannel. A fair comment at the time.

But how wrong she was!

I believe I was meant to be with her for many reasons. The psychic theme seemed to run through her family just as much as mine. - . I was told that my Grandmother on my mum's side had the gift. She could tell when people were pregnant and what sex it was going to be.

As a child, walking with her mother along Narberth high street on the way to the local butcher shop, she suddenly stopped her mother and said they had to wait for the funeral procession to go by before they could move on again. My great grandmother asked her whose funeral was going by because she knew of no one who had passed in their very small, close knit community.

My Grandmother said it was the man who lived two doors away from them. Of course there wasn't a funeral procession and my great grandmother got annoyed at the delay to her very busy day. A few days later the man two doors away passed away and the funeral took place and they stood exactly where my Nan had said to stop and they watched the funeral pass.

Things were indeed working out and my life seemed to have taken a turn for the better at long last. It was in 1992, on a wonderful holiday, that Sarah fell pregnant. We were so happy with the news and, with spring in the air everything seemed right with the world.

One Sunday afternoon about 3 months into the pregnancy, we were out on a warm afternoon picking strawberries when Sarah told me she was feeling pain in her stomach. When we got home she had started to bleed and we rushed off to the hospital.

The miscarriage hit us both hard. Especially Sarah.

It would be a few months later before things started to return to any kind of normality. Life would carry on chugging like a tired steam train for some time before we finally left the tracks of the past behind as best we could.

One afternoon Sarah decided that we should go to a psychic fayre.

I wasn't really sure what to expect.

It made me think of the circus.

We ended up going with my mum to this "fayre" at a Hotel on the outskirts of Portsmouth. There were lots of stalls with various advertising banners and literature, readings, demonstrations and all kinds of spiritual psychic stuff, most of which I had never heard of.

Some Psychics were charging around £25 for a personal reading!

Sarah couldn't resist and I rolled my eyes, standing outside to have another smoke and contemplate my situation and how I could get out of it. I didn't know how I felt about these people.

Con men?

Wackos?

It all felt far too weird and I felt like a square peg in a round hole. Finishing up my cigarette, I decided to grit my teeth and smile politely while my wife enjoyed the rest of the day.

Later that afternoon. It was announced that a popular medium was about to do a demonstration.

Oh great.

At first, I stared at my shoes, thinking they could do with a polish, but somehow as the demonstration went on I became more and more fascinated. Before long we both sat enthralled, listening intently as she went to several people in the audience. They seemed amazed at how much information was coming through for them and how accurate it was.

Then, remarkably, she came to us!

She asked me a question.

Uh?

She asked if I knew someone who had passed away.

They were apparently German.

The name started with an E.

I was rooted to my seat.

I was blown away.

I confirmed this as my grandfather on my mother's side. He was called Ernest, he was a German and he had passed away some years before.

I didn't understand how she could have this information or what it meant.

As if this wasn't enough to have my head spinning, she then also went on to explain that I had lost a close friend in an accident. His name began with an M. He was a tall, blonde and very handsome man and that we were both into a lot of new music at the time of his passing.

I couldn't believe it. That was my friend Mark.

I just sat there with my mouth open, not knowing how to react.

Was she for real?

How did she know so much stuff?

She then said something that shocked and terrified me to the bone. I have never forgotten that moment. It's one of those life changing events that define who you are.

She said that I have been chosen to do spirits work and that one day my life would change. I would be standing up in front of lots of people doing what she was doing right now.

She also said that I will one day change the way that the establishment looks at spiritual connections.

Ok then......

I was just absolutely devastated, despite my skepticism. Sarah laughed and whispered that she must've got me mixed up with someone "psychic" nearby.

I sat there like a rabbit caught in the headlights of an oncoming truck at night. Too frightened to move and too confused to understand.

The medium turned to Sarah. She said that she had a baby in spirit that belonged to us and that he was very happy and was going to grow up on the other side. Sarah looked at her for a moment and understandably, burst into tears.

It was very emotional for both of us and the medium dealt with it very well. She said that she was aware of a little girl with blonde hair sitting in between us.

Wishing us all the best, she finished her reading, making me promise that when spirit came through in a few years that I wouldn't ignore it.

We left afterwards feeling very drained.

I didn't know what to think.

About four years later we went to another psychic fare and the same medium was there. We had taken our daughter… She was sitting between us and had the most beautiful blonde hair which the medium remembered.

Ok, so, she was right about that.

But I still didn't want to believe that she was right about the other future where I was to become a medium.

I put the whole episode behind me and carried on with my life, working at the Continental Ferry Port, pushing pieces of paper around and doing as little as humanly possible. Money was short as always so I also started a part-time job delivering pizzas. Pretty soon this led to an opportunity to drive taxis in the evenings that I wasn't working elsewhere. I became very tired, very quickly.

I was working about seventy hours a week.

After all, I now had a wife and two young children to take care of.

One evening my mum called and told us that there was a very renowned psychic medium showing at the King's Theatre in the centre of town. She had some spare tickets and thought we'd like to go with her.

Oh ok, I guess so, gets me out of the house and I could do with a night off.

I can remember feeling really strange when I went into the theatre. It was a feeling that I have had so often since –a huge feeling of both excitement and pain. We sat down in our designated seats and, for a while, I just watched everyone around the theatre. I could almost see the different personalities out there.

Some people were almost hiding. Others were laughing and joking of things to come, most were just hoping and praying that the medium would eventually come to them.

The Psychic eventually came onto the stage to a round of applause.

I didn't feel right.

I could somehow see someone just behind him. At first it was more that I could sense the spirit of a young girl. She was barely visible next to the psychic, but it was clearly a young girl. He began to ask if anyone in the audience knew of a young girl that had passed away in a house fire. I couldn't believe what I was hearing. It was such a shock that I could see and feel this child he was talking about.

All of a sudden lots of memories started flying into my mind of when I was younger. Seeing James Saunders in my room, the hauntings, the family thread and the previous medium's premonition that made my wife laugh so much at the psychic fayre.

I wasn't sure at the time what set me off, whether it was the overwhelming energy in the room, but I just started to cry.

I couldn't stop.

My mum asked if everything was alright, but I waited until the interval and left the theatre. I couldn't handle it. All I could feel was the overwhelming pain of "loss"

Things got back to normal after a few days and I guess I ignored (again) what had happened. My wife had started to go back to her classes, practicing her psychic medium stuff and doing some tarot readings. I still had mixed feelings, but after the last two events my mind was slowly trying to come to terms with what I felt inside. It seemed to keep coming back to me. There were things happening that I definitely couldn't explain.

Two years later I sat in my taxi and had just about had enough of the pressures of life and work and not ever having any money. My marriage was suffering and I wasn't spending anytime at home. All I did was work 24-7 to pay the bills.

I sat on the Taxi Rank outside a large nightclub at the seafront. I was at the back of a huge queue of cabs waiting in line.

Suddenly I felt a chill. Strange, it was summertime and still very warm. But this chill wasn't the usual kind you get. It went all the way down my left arm. I shut off the music and I'm not sure what I was doing but I asked if anyone was there.

I got a reply.

It was Mark Dryden, my friend who had died so many years before.

He simply said he was with me.

I couldn't believe it. Fear and excitement gripped me at the same time.

I could only hear my own voice, but I knew it was him. Images flashed in my head of him from the past and of him sitting right next to me in the cab.

This was just too freaky.

I faltered, so many thoughts and questions, I asked him, in a trembling voice, if he was ok.

He was, but explained that he had come to see me for a reason. The spirits were worried about me and that I should be careful not to do anything silly.

Like what?

He said that my life would turn out just fine and that I was to take what was going to happen in the next few years on the chin as it was all part of my learning process.

I explained out loud that I was suffering and so tired all the time.

What happened next was one of the most important moments of my life. He showed me where he was in the spirit world.

It was the most wonderful thing I have ever seen or felt. He showed me the countryside I used to play in on our holidays in Wales. He showed me images of me and him with lots of people I didn't recognise, but somehow felt I knew. We were lying in a field with the warm sun washing over our faces whilst we talked and laughed.

I felt so relaxed at that point. He played music I have never heard before and showed me a different scene.

It was night time. There was a full moon and we were beside a lake. There were different sized boats moored to a long jetty with a light wind gently clinking the masts and sails. It was such an amazing place and my relaxation turned to contentment.

The feelings that I was having, the sensations that made me feel so relaxed were, as Mark explained, how it feels to be Spirit.

I can only describe it as that same feeling you get when you first kiss a partner that you really love, and also kind of like the feeling you get when with your closest friends and they make you laugh so much you think you might be sick!

I will never forget that moment. Once it had passed I was in a new state of mind just bubbling to the surface. It was a new goal I was working towards as I said farewell to my friend and thanked him for the wonders he'd shown me.

That goal was the ultimate we can aspire to in life which I hadn't realised until that very moment.

Quite simply, it was a place in Heaven.

Chapter Five

SPANISH LESSONS

Jan 2000

MY WIFE AND I were having problems with our marriage. No blame is directed here, we just weren't getting on and we were drifting further and further apart. I had decided to go with her to see a marriage guidance councellor - something that I was never going to be comfortable with, but for the sake of the relationship it was worth it. The councellor had been recommended by a family friend and we both went together for the first few times. It was all very enlightening and helpful in its own way, but it wasn't bringing us closer together by any stretch of the imagination. We then decided on something a bit more radical and go to the councellor separately. It was more of a one-on-one personal therapy. For me, at such a critical time, it became more of a voyage of self-discovery than relationship mending.

I used the time to tell her all the things I had been feeling and, more importantly, question the things that went on in my head, the psychic phenomena that was occurring around me and the "supernatural" events that had sprung up over the last few weeks. I felt like my head may explode any moment.

What did all this mean?

What was I to do?

How should I feel?

She listened to me for about 3 months and then out of nowhere produced a business card with the details of some place called "The Holistic Centre" in Portsmouth. It was a place for holistic and psychic therapy, specialising in teaching people with psychic or potential mediumship skills.

I thought about it long and hard, and put the card away. It was all getting a bit too scary for me.

My wife, children and I decided to take advantage of an offer that was going around work. You could fly standby with a certain airline, anywhere in the world for £100 each including taxes. I thought it would be wrong to miss an opportunity like this, plus I felt an amazing urge to head to California again. We decided to go and booked it.

Of course, we all had a nice time. Funnily enough, I still thought that this was a make or break holiday for our marriage. It seemed to be a way of getting back to basics with my wife and time for a little bonding.

During the holiday we stayed at Lake Tahoe, Nevada.

One restless night, about three am, whilst everyone was fast asleep, I took a blanket from the closet and went off in our hire car. I wasn't sure what I was going to do or where I was going, but I found myself under a blanket by the shore for a good five hours watching the sun come up and thinking about all I had been through in these recent years. I had lots of decisions to make regarding the direction my life had to head in. I needed to make some dramatic changes. I'd no idea where this was going or what I was to do. I rummaged in my rucksack for a can of drink.

In the bottom of the sack was the card that I had been given by the therapist.

Did I put that in there?

I was sure that I had left it on my desk at home.

If this was a sign then it was punching me square on the chin.

I had no other choice as far as I was concerned and when we got back from holiday I immediately called them up.

I explained myself on the phone, feeling very foolish. They were very helpful and said that they did courses on a Thursday night for forty weeks. At the time I was still doing shift work at the ferry port and knew that I could only attend bi-weekly at best.

Unfortunately, they couldn't accommodate, so I went into work and, as I was a shift leader, decided that I would let my other shift members go home on a late shift early during the week and I, in turn, would be able to go every Thursday early.

"What was I doing on a Thursday night?" they asked.

"Well, I'm. Err…. well…. Ummmmmmmm,"

What should I say?

It came to me.
"Spanish lessons."
Smooooooth!

It seemed like a reasonable excuse. They seemed to accept it. It was, after all, an international trade route we dealt with. It looked like I was a company go-getter. They liked that.

So I set about getting there every Thursday. I wasn't sure what I expected to find. Even being a taxi driver part time. I still had never heard of this place and certainly never took anyone there. I waited outside after going to the pub for a drink. As I entered I noticed that it was a converted pub. with no drink.

With no drink! It was built over two floors and a curtain separated a hall that was used as a spiritualist church and we were to be sat on chairs in a circle for 2 hours. That first night there were around twenty two of us. Most of us had come on our own, and there was a cross section of people. Some old ladies, two young men about 18, some middle aged married men and women as well, and also a couple of tarot readers and psychics that were there to brush up on their skills. I met some of them during the time that we were being seated. I sat between a nurse and a computer engineer. Then in walked a man called Mark. He was quite tall and very thin and had a camp way about him, but also a very quiet demeanour. He opened up by telling us what we were to expect over the next ten weeks. He also added that most of the group would be whittled down through no fault of our own over the next four blocks of ten week courses, and that this experience will change our lives forever. I did wonder what the bloody hell he was going on about and whether I should leg it there and then as this was getting a little bit freaky for me already, and I had nearly a year of this to go.

Oh how right Mark was on that first day.

Over the coming weeks we all became quite good friends. A few people thought they were the dogs at being psychic and healing people and it was there that I learned so many lessons about people in this field of work. Some I couldn't stand for being so up themselves. A lady arrived on the second week called Vicky. I hated her on sight. She pulled up outside in a sports car and was dressed to the nines. I thought she was a bit of a snob at first. She has turned out to be one of my best friends. Naturally funny and has such an amazing personality. I warmed to her as the weeks went by. Some of the stuff we had to do put us in fits of laughter.

The first thing we had to do was to sit in the most uncomfortable chairs you have ever felt in your life in a circle with some terrible music wailing painfully in the backround. A sort of whale song.

Without whales.

Or tune.

Mmmm.

I wasn't sure what to expect. We were then taught how to sit in a certain (uncomfortable) position. We were then shown how we were to meditate. It went like this: Breathe in, hold for three seconds, Breathe out. Do that three times.

I was pretty sure I already knew how to breathe. I had done it before.

Then we had to think about 17 different parts of out body whilst breathing in and out. (Not even the interesting ones!) We were to relax each individual body part with each breathe - Blowing out any stress. I think we spent more time worrying about whether we were doing it right than actually getting round to the point of relaxing. It was all a bit too weird, too structured. We had to imagine a golden ball of light in front of us and breathe in strands of light into different parts of our throat and chest, blowing out different coloured smoke.

I nearly left halfway through the first week.

But I persevered. Over the coming weeks, our tutors prophecy came true and we were whittled down to just eight of us. To be fair, it was fun most of the time and also quite productive. But some of it was utter gibberish as far as I was concerned. I didn't like being told how to relax in such a regimented way and were suppose to do these long and exhausting exercises at home. I just didn't have the time.

Or the energy.

…and I certainly didn't want to buy any Whale music!

I went every week however, doing what I had to do and learnt a lot in the process. I might not have enjoyed their methods, but it was helping in many ways.

I still kept all this from everyone at work. As far as they were concerned I had six months of intensive Spanish language lessons. Well, as you can imagine, I got my just desserts when I was once asked to the counter to use my newly acquired skill and speak with Spanish lorry driver!!!

Of course, I couldn't speak a word of it. Everyone wanted to know why I couldn't even hold a basic conversation with the guy after all those lessons. I made some lame excuse about regional dialects and hoped for the best. It seemed to work, thankfully.

If only they had known!

A few months later something happened that scared me. I didn't know at the time that I was a few days from leaving my wife and starting a chain of events that would lead me to sitting here, in my new home, with my new wife and writing this book.

I went to Sainsbury's to buy something to cook for dinner.

I left in the car, put Nirvana on the stereo and turned it up really loud and went to the store. On the way back I felt really strange. There was someone with me. I had just completed twenty weeks at the Holistic Centre and was coming along quite well. I had already done my first church meeting and it had gone a lot better than I ever could have anticipated. I realized that Mark, my friend who passed away in the accident, was with me again, but I didn't want to talk to anyone from spirit. I was not in a right frame of mind at the time to want to connect with upstairs. I got home and opened the front door and my wife just went mental and started backing away from the front door shouting" Back off, you're scaring me." I asked her what the bloody hell she was going on about and she explained that a young man had followed me into the house and was very agitated. He told her that I was ignoring him and he needed to say something. He then went on to explain to my wife to tell me that everything was going to be ok and not to lose faith. Get through the next few days and it will all work out in the end. That night I was lying in bed. I couldn't sleep. I looked over at the kid's bedroom door when suddenly it just started banging against the frame over and over. It was practically coming off its hinges. It scared me to death. I turned over to wake my wife, but of course, she was already awake. She didn't seem perturbed by the occurrence. I asked her what it was and she said quite calmly it was spirit again. I jumped up and went into the kid's room to find out if they were ok. To my relief they were both sound asleep. Then it started again, the banging. My wife shouted at whoever it was to stop the incessant noise. It did.

At that point, something clicked.

I practically ran out of the house, got into the car and drove away. It seemed like my brain was splitting in two, my life careering dangerously off the rails. I knew spirit was warning me of the imminent changes that were taking place. Whatever choices I had, whatever decisions I made would be with me for the rest of my life. I had to do what I thought was right.

I drove on into the early hours, searching my soul and making my choice. I knew I would pay a terrible price and I would never be the same, but I knew my destiny lay down a different road. I won't go into detail about reasoning and how I felt, especially with regards to my children and how it would affect them. That is something that I have to live with. And something I hope they one day will understand.

Two days later I left my wife and started a new life on my spiritual journey.

Chapter Six

HOUSE OF CARDS

TOWARDS THE END of my course at the Holistic Centre. I knew I should get my name out there and get some private readings under my belt.

It started very well. I was using Tarot a lot at the time, finding it a helpful tool, especially for a beginner like me. I began with family and friends, assuming that it was a good place to start. For a while it was extremely beneficial. Although there were many things to learn whilst using Tarot, it didn't take me long to pick up what each card meant and how it related to the person receiving the information. I had a little folder which was – to all intents and purposes – my cheat sheet, which I could refer to if the information on the cards gave me pause for thought or threw me in any way.

In a way, to begin with, the cards were a psychological crutch. They helped me to focus my attention and added weight to whatever information I had for the person sat opposite me. The problem was that as time went on, I felt more and more uncomfortable about using the cards. I really didn't know what it was. I got to the point where I was doing as many as three or four readings a week with the cards – all of which went very well. But I wasn't feeling at all fulfilled.

I just couldn't grasp what it was that bothered me.

Then one day it occurred to me. I was sitting down with a family at their home one evening. They had invited me round to do some Tarot readings. They had heard about me from a friend of theirs who had told them that I was very accurate. I did enjoy the fact that my name was getting around and people wanted to see me.

After the first two or three readings a lady came in. I then started to shuffle the cards for her. She sat opposite me and apart from being very gorgeous looking; she brought with her a very strong sadness. I went on to explain what I was about to do and if she could ask a question in head. I asked her not to tell me and she said she wouldn't. I laid the cards out in front of me.

They had absolutely no meaning whatsoever. The cards were just in such a mess. No reason to them at all. I had got quite good at reading the cards by then, so to have ten different cards with no rhyme or reason behind them. It just stumped me. I just sat and stared at them. She asked me if everything was ok. I hesitantly and with a stutter, explained to her that the cards she had dealt meant nothing. I didn't need to ask her if they meant anything to her because they were just all over the place.

It was then that I heard it. It was the voice of a young child. He giggled in my ear. Freaky! I thought it might be my guides laughing at me as I was stuttering by then. I kind of just waved the voice away and then decided to re-shuffle the deck and lay it out. By this time the lady in front of me was getting very nervous. I think I would if I didn't know what was going on and a psychic was sitting in front of me shooing something that I couldn't see, away. I must have looked like a right loony. Bless her.

It was then that the voice came back and told me that I was talking to the ladies son. He had recently passed over and she was there to hear from him. Spirit had arranged it and thought it best to kill two birds with one stone. He came through with such strength that I then decided it was time to put the cards away and connect this lady with her son.

After around twenty minutes the lady got up and came round to other side of the table. She then gave me the biggest hug. She said that she wanted to hear from her Son and that she had hoped that I was a medium as well as a card reader. She said that I was amazing and she couldn't have dreamed of a better outcome to help her come to terms with her loss.

I did another connection after she left and then I decided to go home. I sat in my car and thought about what had just occurred. I then decided to take a drive to Portsdown Hill. This is an area that has amazing views across Portsmouth from quite a high vantage point. I parked the car and sat with some quiet music on. It was while I sat there that I realized what was wrong with me. I just didn't want to tell peoples fortune anymore. After that incident with the lady and her son I just didn't have the need to tell the next person whether they were going to meet Mr. Right or Mr. Right for now! It wasn't fulfilling enough. What I had done back there was an amazing feeling. I had been the one to connect with her son and make her loss a little easier to deal with.

I had learned the difference between healers, Tarot readers and mediums at the Holistic Centre. I thought that I would try Tarot as I was getting good at it. But that night I realized. If I could make someone feel healed about their loss and get a connection that actually helps. Then I wanted to be a medium.

I was meant to be a medium.

At least until the next time the self doubt crept in!

Chapter Seven

EGO THAT WAY
OR EGO THE OTHER

DURING MY TIME at the Holistic training centre - even with the dubious music and uncomfortable chairs - I still felt that the experience was good for me as a novice medium. As I mentioned, most of the teachings went completely over my head, what with the whale mating song and learning how to breathe in and out. At one point we were even involved in exercises that involved standing in the centre of the room pretending we were skiing down a mountainside in front of twenty other confused and sniggering students!

I must admit that I was glad when the course ended. It was supposed to be over forty odd weeks. We had just completed our thirtieth and they had covered everything from spirit connection to Tarot and healing. The teacher became a great influence during the course. Despite his orders from his employer to follow the curriculum, he managed to bend the rules when he could – positively snapping them in half on occasion when he thought it was important to do so.

Even he even found a lot of what we were doing a bit bizarre!

At the end of each month we would sit in a group with other students and do a sort of group Spirit connection. These turned out to be very informative and quite illuminating. Some of the others would bring their own style and experiences to it. We would all retire to the pub afterwards, drink a few pints and share our thoughts and interests. The landlord would cast a weary eye over us. He knew us as the weirdo's from the centre across the road. He thought we were on a day release from the local mental institute, but stayed polite in case we were drooling and dangerous.

One week, our tutor was out sick and it transpired that the owner of the centre would be teaching us that day.

We were doing Psychometry.

This is where a piece of jewelery belonging to each of us is put on a tray and we are to pick it up, touch it and from the vibes, tell everyone a little about the owner of the item.

It got to my turn. I seemed to get something immediately. I was halfway through explaining to one of the other people that her grandfather had passed when I was rudely told to place the item back so they could move on. The lady asked the owner if we could carry on and that she really wanted to hear from her grandfather. The owner told her to please be quiet because the evening wasn't long enough for individual reading.

I thought that was the whole point and decided after that night that if I was forced to work with the owner of the Holistic Centre again, I wouldn't bother.

A week later we found out that, indeed, we would have him again. Our tutor was leaving and was told that we would be working with the centers owner again.

We all decided to leave.

On the last day we were there the tutor told me, just before he left for his new job, that I was an outstanding medium and would like to see me stage or appearing in churches and community centres. This comment threw me completely. After that my head couldn't fit through the door. It gave me the boost I needed, knowing he thought so much of my ability and that I was really good at this and it was then that I decided to get out there and start doing readings.

The problem with that is I hadn't remembered to leave something very important behind me when I left.

My ego.

Chapter Eight

SITTING ON A GOLD MINE

SO THERE I am, sitting outside my mum's house in Gosport, Hampshire. It's raining, cold and I am waiting for the guy who lives next door to come home so he can give me the spare key to her house.

I only have four pounds to my name and everything I own in the world is in a tatty old duffel bag that I am using as a makeshift seat. The airport tags on the bag say,

Toronto to Gatwick. 23/01/2001.

A few hours previous I was on a plane coming home from Canada – alone. I had phoned my mother from Toronto with some of the last Canadian dollars I had asked if I could stay at her house for the time being, until I got myself sorted. She was on a world trip, at that time in Australia. Of course, she said yes straight away and I had somewhere to rest and collect my thoughts.

So how did this all come about?

Well, let me start at the beginning.

1ˢᵗ April 2001

My mum's 50ᵗʰ birthday party took place at the Police Club in Kingston Crescent, Portsmouth. I was having a great time, standing by the dance floor, quite drunk and wobbling along to the beats of the latest chart nonsense. Then came the part of the evening that every single person dreads. The DJ puts on a slow song and you feel obliged to ask any female in the general vicinity to dance – lest you look like the biggest loser since the guy who invented square wheels. Well, I tried and asked a few girls to dance. Got rejected. Drunk another beer and resided to my fate.

Then I saw her.

She was standing over by the bar. She was wearing an Armani dress and diamonds. The most gorgeous woman I had ever seen. She looked like Angelina Jolie.

If I had died then and there I would have been content that I had at least laid my eyes on such a beauty. I was definitely in some kind of dream sequence from a movie. The room went misty around her and all sound seemed to drown away.

All I could see was her.

I took another swig of my drink and staggered over.

"Would you like to dance?" I muttered, feeling the heat in my face…either from fear or beer.

"I would love to"

Eh? Did she just say yes?

A few months later the two of us decided to move in together.

We were just friends at the time. At least, that's what it was to begin with.

We just happened to sleep in the same bed.

It was about then I fell in love with her. Hook, line and sinker. The complexities of our relationship are something I will not bore you with, but it's important for you, good reader, to note that I was blinded by emotion I had never felt before and it is partly that emotion that led to a downward spiral that took me to places I never should have been and thoughts I should never allowed myself to even contemplate. But I am, after all, only human.

We moved to a basement apartment by the sea front. We chose that flat as it was close to the pubs and clubs and also to the shops. It was a nice place. We settled in and made it as homely as possible with the collective goods we had brought from our own homes.

A few weeks later the trouble started. We were in the bed dropping off nicely to sleep when we were suddenly awoken by a very loud scratching sound from the door of our room. Shocked and scared, Natalie asked what it was. I was tired and had little interest. I said it was probably mice. Natalie correctly pointed out that if it was mice, then they had to be genetically altered mice with ten foot claws.

I did a vague attempt at being a good boyfriend and got up to investigate. There was nothing there.

A couple of nights later the door opened, on its own and the kitchen light came on. Natalie called to me to make her a drink and turned over. I then said ok honey. She immediately jumped up out of her skin as she didn't realize I was still next to her. She had thought I was in the kitchen getting a drink. Other things started to happen over the course of a month or two. We both started to hate sleeping in the bedroom. It had become so cold, even though it was summer. We decided that we would move to the front room and buy a sofa bed. We would sleep there instead. One night I went to the bathroom and had the shock of my life. There was a girl staring at me. She reached out with both arms and shouted. I filled my underwear and ran out. I also never felt comfortable in the house on my own. Neither did Natalie. She sometimes would work in different parts of the country. She was a salesperson for a brewing company. So she would often find herself having to drive to Cornwall and stay over night as the drive would be too much in one day. It got to a point where I would take the day off and drive her to Falmouth and back. Eleven hour drive, just so I could spend time out of the flat. I am a medium and speak to spirits all the time. But this still made me very nervous. I didn't like the atmosphere in the house. Some nights my girlfriend would come home fairly late. After a long day at work I would fix her dinner and then run her bath and put candles round the edge so she could undress and jump straight in. The trouble was she didn't feel at all comfortable in the bath and would be out of there in around five minutes. She would often ask me to stay with her, which of course I had no problems with! One Saturday night we decided to have a whole weekend in. So we settled down with food and movies. During the night she looked over and saw a man in the corner. Suddenly the end of the quilt rose up by about a foot, and she felt someone tickling her feet. It was one of those things that just freaks you out. Once we had her ex husbands African Grey parrot stay over and we went out for the night. We arrived home in the early hours and he was sitting on the floor of the cage squawking really loudly and most of his feathers had turned white. We decided that we couldn't wait to move after that. One morning a taxi collected me from my flat to take me to work. He asked if I lived at 21a. I confirmed this and he told me that a girl had been murdered there a few months before we moved in. Great!

The next part of the story almost happened in fast-forward. Like a blur to me now.

Natalie had an idea.

She thought we should move to Canada. The plan was to do readings over there. Not readings for two or three people in a living room or even a small community hall environment. This was a BIG plan. Theatres and Auditoriums. She had connections. She had the Business degree. It would be a cinch.

Four thousand tickets sales a night at twenty dollars a pop. Her notion was that I could do three a week and within a year we would be millionaires.

Brilliant!

Rich beyond our wildest dreams…all because I can talk to dead people!

I was swept away on the tide of her enthusiasm and knowledge, dollar signs ker-chinged in my brain. At no point did I question the logistics, complexities or idiocy of the plan. There were no morals or ethics entering into the equation. At the time, it was my way out. Out of the rat race, out of the boredom of work and into Natalie's heart.

And we were gonna get rich…..and quick!

I would be able to give her everything she ever wanted and more!

I decided to hand my notice in at work and subsequently sold everything we owned in a car boot sale. We converted it all to Canadian Dollars and she left for Canada nine days earlier than me to get started and set the wheels in motion.

It was going well. I even had a stroke of luck over the money conversion. I found myself eight hundred Canadian dollars richer. We talked everyday about my impending fame and fortune. In truth, it was only my way of keeping her. I just needed to be with her in a different place. I couldn't wait.

She found my first venue - The Norman Rothstein Theatre in the Jewish district of Vancouver, British Columbia.

I was so excited and missing her so much. On the morning of the November 10th, I left my mum's house and said goodbye to her for what felt like a move that would see me living and working in Canada for the rest of my life. I even told her to book her flight in a year to come to our wedding ceremony.

I got to Gatwick airport and as usual when I am traveling by airplane arrived at least five hours early. I got to the airport to find a huge queue at check-in already for the plane to Vancouver. A young man walked along the queue and gave out a leaflet saying that the airline taking me had ceased trading and that we were to find alternate means of transport. What kind of transport? Sail or maybe I should swim!! I then had to wait 24 hours at Gatwick after purchasing a new ticket from another airline to Vancouver via Houston TX. USA. It cost me three hundred and fifty pounds which is roughly eight hundred Canadian dollars.

Oh the irony!!!!!

Someone, somewhere was trying to tell me something. I should have listened.

I arrived in Vancouver 51hours after my original flight should have left and I was met at the airport by Natalie. I was tired, miserable and needed a shower... but the woman of my dreams was here and we were about to start a new life together with all the pressures and stress of my past well and truly behind me.

The best laid plans and all that!

5ᵗʰ December 2001

I arrived at the theatre ready to do my show. My first in front of an audience, which was more than ten people in a living room. To say I was nervous is the biggest understatement. How I managed not to throw up is anyone's guess. Adrenaline soon took over. I was starting to feel pumped. The nerves were being replaced by exhilaration.

During my short stay in Vancouver I had done some small, impromptu readings and the memory of these successful outings certainly gave me an extra boost (more on those later in the book)

Natalie had me fitted up with a brand new dark suit. It cost about a thousand dollars. I had never worn a suit that cost that much! But I did look the bees' knees.

Here I was, in Canada doing a show in front of what I thought to be about 500 people.

"Start small" I had been told many times before. Well, hey! This venue was smallish, right? I wanted four thousand people. A room of five hundred was chicken feed.

I was starting to feel cocky.

I was losing my nerves and replacing it with some false confidence.

Maybe it was the suit. Maybe it was Natalie's smile.

I had picked some songs to be played whilst I waited in the wings with a bottle of strong Dutch courage. The music got louder and I walked on stage…

To a total of only 42 people!

I just stood there. Like an idiot in a very expensive suit that cost more than we were getting from the damn ticket sales. I had spent more time making sure that the music had been right and that I came on at the right place – I had even made sure that the lighting was subtle enough. I didn't think of anything past the small introduction that I had memorized.

42 people?

My heart sank and my stomach rumbled.

42 people.

I had to get in check. I had to sort out my disappointment and growing pessimism before the only people that had turned up got up and went home.

Don't look back and just get on with it…

So I began.

My first connection that evening was to an older lady who had lost her husband. I got the name of her husband and her name straight away, which was a great start. I then went on to describe him, the condition of which he passed and some acquaintances they both knew.   It all looked promising. She said thank you aloud after the reading and I began to relax a little and concentrate on the job at hand…this was going to be a piece of cake!

Then of course, the worse thing happened.

I went blank.

I had no connections

Nothing came through at all.

Zip

Nada.

Mr. Big Time had fallen over after the first connection. The thing is, looking back, I had thought I was the best thing ever in all those living rooms I had done in the past. I assumed it would just flow and I would have a great connection for everyone.

But no.

Welcome to the real world, Pal!

It seemed like an eternity for something to happen. It was as if someone had rushed on the stage and pulled my pants down. In fact, that would have at least detracted from the fact that my mind had shut off completely.

I waited for a while longer, pacing up and down and straining for messages.

It was such a relief when finally something started to come through. It was for a gentleman sitting with his wife. I had a man through whose name was Earl. He was quite flamboyant and very camp. He used to be a dancer and something to do with cruise ships. A man in the audience I pointed too didn't understand any of it!! He had no idea who I was talking about. Thoughts of failure were running through my head again by that point.

Someone get me a noose!

I didn't have the knowledge I have now. If you're not getting anything then you wait. It's not an exact science. It's not a script and it's not always going to work. It's also only going to happen on spirits timescale. I called an early break and practically ran off the stage. I got to my dressing room and cried. I tried to get my friends to go down and cancel the rest of the evening. They could say I had fallen over or something.

Message from Upstairs - "No way. Get your arse down there and get on with it", I had to go out there and tell them myself.

I came onto the stage again feeling like hammered crap. I had let everyone down. I had let my partner down and all the people that had come for a message.

I couldn't feel any worse than I felt right now.

Mr. Big Shot had been taught a lesson in humility.

The sound people in their booth put on another song for my big entrance. I shouted up to them, asking them turn on the house lights and turn off the music.

Upstairs came through again "get down off the stage, get a chair and sit in front of the audience" huh?

I wasn't sure where they were heading with all this.

But as usual it was the right thing to do.

I just talked with the audience.

Something interesting happened. The gentleman I had spoken to before the break had made a phone call at his wife's insistence to one of his real estate clients. He had had dinner with him a few days previously. It turned out that the client's partner was called Earl and he used to be a dancer. They had traveled on cruise ships for every vacation since being together for 40 years. He had recently passed over.

I felt a slight weight off my shoulders. Only slight, but it sure helped.

I was then told by upstairs that I would allow people to ask questions and I would answer them to my best ability. I wasn't getting anything else through. I was stressed, upset and feeling totally humiliated. It seemed like a good direction to go in.

Just me

The rest of the evening went amazingly well. One old lady got up halfway through and I thought she was going to go home. I asked her if she was ok. She said she couldn't hear me properly and had to move closer.

That made my day.

At the end I asked them all to take their ticket money home with them as I felt they hadn't got what they had paid for… As I finished up they all stood and gave me a standing ovation.

ME!

It was probably one of the best memories I have of that trip. It made me feel so wonderful to be accepted by them, despite an evening that I would say was not entirely satisfactory! I learnt many lessons that evening. Most were a slap in the face. What the audience taught me warms my heart to this day.

It's never about how many show up to these venues. It's about the reason they show up. If there are one thousand or ten, the people that come are meant to be there. You have to get on with what you booked the venue for in the first place. No matter how badly I felt, I must've helped in some small way.

I want to thank all those people that came that night.

When I got back home everything had changed.

More importantly at the time, everything had changed for Natalie too. Not a great deal was said about the venue. In fact we spoke little of anything relevant to that subject at all.

She became increasingly hostile towards me over the next few days – which then went into weeks.

What had I done?

Around Christmas time she announced she was going to Toronto to spend the holiday with her family… and that she was going on her own.

Despite my best protestations and questions, I finally saw her away at the airport, trying hard to be strong, fighting the twisting in my stomach. I was completely lost and helpless.

I didn't understand why this was happening to me.

I had given up so much to be with her.

Blinded by my feelings for her, I still didn't understand.

It was around that time that I called my dad to talk to him. I had checked our bank account and we had no money. My dad told me that I wasn't allowed to spend Christmas on my own and that he and his wife, Rachel, would send me some money to get to California so I could spend Christmas with my sister. She had not long moved to California and was staying with her husband's family in Hollister, near San Jose.

Talking with my friend Dawn about my plan, she kindly offered to drive me to the airport in Seattle, Washington...

I said goodbye to her and said that I would be back to see her again soon. In truth, I never thought I would see her again.

I spoke to Natalie often, yet the conversations were strained and polite at best.

I decided to find out what was happening with us.

I just had to.

On New Years day I decided to take a bus to Toronto, Ontario. I didn't even realize the distance I would be covering. It is around 3000 miles and 61 hours on the bus!

That bus journey was amazing, yet I missed so much of it due to my head spinning, purely due to the delay it created in being with Natalie, coupled with exhaustion from a four-day bus ride itself and a numb bottom.

I did, however, get to realize a lifelong dream of crossing the USA.

I saw the most incredible sights from the bus window.

My main memory is standing in the Nevada desert at 3.30 am. Never had I seen so many stars in the sky.

...And never had I felt as alone as I did on that trip.

Life was just carrying on in a surreal way. Towards the end of the journey, the whole world appeared to me as a smudged oil painting. I finally arrived in Toronto and met up briefly with Natalie.

She wasn't pleased to see me.

She doesn't want me here. What did I expect?

I swallowed back my tears and made the decision that it was time to call it a day.

The hardest thing I ever did but one of the most sensible.

So I ended up with my tail between my legs, slumped on a duffel bag in the pouring rain waiting for a key. It was my own fault.

I had broken all my own rules and betrayed my own beliefs.

I was broken-hearted and full of self-loathing.

The same things went through my head....and they would for a long time:

What the hell was I thinking?
I wasn't a Medium....
And would never try to be again.

Lesson from this:

Please never make this work about the money and the fame. It's very easy to fall into that trap. Spirit will help as much as they can financially. But the money has to be the last thing that this work is about. They will give you a swift kick up the arse and put you in your place if you do. If you do the work to the best of your ability and for the right reasons. Then you will be looked after.

Chapter Nine

A BRAVE NEW WORLD

AFTER THE EVENTS that took place in Canada, I didn't want to be a medium. I hated the thought of doing anything related to the world of spirit after such bad memories of what had happened. I had so many questions in the grey matter between my eyes. Why had Spirit sent me all the way to Canada? Not only to fail but also to lose the love of my life? I was also so annoyed with myself for the way I had approached it – throwing my own morals and ethics to the wind, annoyed with Natalie for leading me to that and, most of all, heart-broken for having to make the decision to end it between us, despite her femme fatale ways.

It didn't matter how much of my life revolved around the world of Spirit and how much it meant to me…..things had changed. I knew I had over-stepped whatever mark was there. The crew in Head Office was not happy with me.

By the way. As we are going to be with each other for this book, when I refer to the "Crew" or "Head Office" I mean Spirit.

Anyway, I put it to the back of my mind, confident that I was doing the right thing.

Being a Psychic was like standing in front of a charging bull with my ass painted red…..stupid, humiliating, and helpful to no one.

Never again.

I spent about three days of the coming weeks even going as far as to think of ending it. I know? Over what? Well, Natalie was gone and I would never get her back or see her again. That was the hardest part knowing that. I did wonder for a while whether it was worth going on. I was sat in my mum's lounge with a bottle of whisky, feeling way too sorry for myself. I also wondered what the hell I was supposed to do now. I didn't want to be a medium. I would be the laughing stock of everyone I had told my plans too.

I would also have to face everyone. Not as a world famous medium but as a taxi driver again. How would I be able to live with that?

I finished the bottle of whisky and went to bed. During the night I had a dream. My friend Mark came through and shouted at me. He told me to stop feeling sorry for myself and to get my life sorted. Spirit would help me out on this situation and I would find myself out of the miserable faze I was going through, soon enough. Give us a little time. And, don't do anything stupid.!!!

The next morning, with a raging hangover, I remembered what had been said. I couldn't believe that I had been thinking of doing myself in over love. It was still a raw feeling but nothing should ever have persuaded me to go that far. It was time to sort my head out and get back to the real world.

I decided that I had to get a job. That is, of course, after many days of daytime television and snack food.

What job could I get into….I thought about all the things I had ever wanted to do when I was younger..? Astronaught was a very remote possibility. It would be good just to be the first fat man on the moon.

I had thought seriously about getting back into the shipping business. I had the experience and knowledge……the trouble is, I had the hatred for it too. I telephoned a few companies and got nowhere. It was a bad time of year for hiring.

Ok. That was that idea out the window, down the street and over the horizon in a fast car.

What next?

Well, I eventually decided I needed a job that didn't have too much stress or long hours. A job I could do for now until I worked out where my future lay.

Some psychic huh?

That's an important thing about being so in touch with the world of spirit – they never give away anything that is going to happen. Many people assume a Psychic Medium can tell the future. I, myself, have been asked to do readings, only to find that they were under the impression I could tell what would happen to them in the future.

You just have to realize that they are there and taking care of you. That should be enough to get you by.

I decided that I should maybe get back into taxi driving as I had done it for quite a few years - part time.

I didn't think I would ever get back into doing readings for people or involving myself in Psychic matters again

The memories of Canada were far too raw and painful.

I telephoned my old driving boss, Rose, and she told me that she would keep an eye out among the cabbies for owners that needed a night driver.

She telephoned me a few days later and said that a friend of hers was after a dependable person (me?) for the twilight hours driving his taxi, and that I should give him a call.

I started driving again about a week later.

Things were going quite well. Rose and I were really old buddies and she told me one evening that she needed a lodger - someone to rent a room in her house. Thinking about it, I didn't want to outstay my welcome at mums, so I moved in.

That's when everything changed, again!

It's very difficult to explain my reasons, but the need to share my connections began to come back. Stronger than ever.

I think after a while the pain and problems that had crushed my spirit began to fade. I had ripped myself down and pushed my natural leanings away, trying desperately to come to terms with my shame, anger and loss that I had felt.

In part, the family and friends I had around me filled me with confidence almost every day, holding me aloft while I was drowning and, more importantly, they believed in me.

They knew who I was

....and what I was capable of.

Just me?

I started to come back from wherever I was.

The crew upstairs obviously wasn't prepared to let me lie down and give up either.

It's like they were pushing me.

Ushering me towards the doorway.

Maybe it wasn't over just yet.

I was looking at a brave new world. It was scary – I was nervous, but there was something that was spurring me on.

It felt right.

I suppose, deep down, my calling was there. I was still a medium at heart even if I didn't rate my abilities that highly. I would never be able to get away from it. It was my calling in life to help people.

I decided I still needed a lot of practice. So I decided to put the feelers out and give out a card to people with my details on it. I thought at the time that I wasn't a good enough medium to even consider some kind of charge. Especially after the lessons I had learnt. Deciding to do readings for free, it seemed like the best course of action and I would rely on spirit to help me financially. Plus, if I sucked at it they couldn't put the blame on me. I wasn't making money out of it so that line of cynicism was out the window.

I got some cards designed and took them to the printers. I was told that it would cost £110 for 1000 cards. I had a bit of a shock so I put down a £25 deposit and thought that I would try and earn the other £85 on the Saturday night working on the taxis. That Saturday I bought a ticket for the National Lottery and checked my numbers without much thought. It was incredible!

I got four numbers and it paid out £85!

I have been told over the years through Spirit that everything we think of as coincidence is not. It is all meant to be. Destiny if you can call it that. I dished out the cards over the coming weeks. I got several offers to come to peoples houses and did some amazing connections.

It wasn't for a few months till one night I did a reading at a house in Portsmouth. It went amazingly well. I was thanked for doing it but something was niggling at me. I wasn't being paid for this work. People would tell me that it was a gift from God and should be free. Well, so is an interior designer's flair, but they don't do that for free. The problem with being a medium is people almost always assume that if you are charging you must be a charlatan. Its word of mouth and peoples testimonials that seem to make people realise that you are not just on a wallet emptying connathon! People are reluctant to go to some unknown medium and pay, not knowing if they can deliver the goods or not…..but then, I would never charge if they weren't happy…..A plumber fixes the pipes and we assume he will charge, regardless. He must be good otherwise he wouldn't get business. People are happy to assume this because it's a tangible, obvious "thing" if you think it's a good enough job. I wouldn't charge too much, but I was feeling very poor. Some weeks I would do a whole five nights of connections at people's houses all over Hampshire. Then I would work the weekend to pay for the taxi hire. I didn't have any money at all left over to live on.

I needed to charge only as much as I would make working in the taxi, no more or I felt the kick up the backside I got from Spirit. . I didn't think that this would cause a problem and it didn't. I was feeling quite happy for a while, covering my costs and still helping people the best way I knew how.

Rose went away to South Africa for a two week holiday. She came back in the October. She had managed to get a nasty cough. We thought she had some sort of disease or nasty bug and the doctors did lots of tests. She got really sick around Christmas when I went off to California for Christmas to see my sister. She went for more tests after I got back to England. She had been diagnosed with lung cancer and brain cancer.

She passed away on August 23rd.

She had her faculties about her right up till when she passed. I felt like I had lost a mother when Rose had passed as we were so close. Before she crossed over, I sat at the end of her bed. She knew she was going to pass that night.

It was a Friday and I was going to be heading off to work in the Taxi. She asked me lots of questions about what she should expect when she died. It was very sad to hear, but I told her what I knew. I said she wouldn't be scared and that she would be met by someone she knew and also by my twin brother so she would see a face she knew on the other side. She would also be met by her guides who would help her through the transition. While talking to her I asked her if she would send me sign to let me know that she crossed over ok and that she was happy where she was. She asked me what I wanted and I told her a feather like the one in Forest Gump. She said she could go one better and send me red feathers. She had been to Las Vegas once on holiday and she loved the big red feathers that the Vegas show girls wear.

She passed away in her sleep that night.

I waited a week for my sign. I had almost given up hope when, on the morning of her funeral, a postcard dropped through the door from my friend, Sue. She was in Italy and she had lit a candle in a church in Rome for Rose. On the Postcard was a cherub and it had wings made of RED FEATHERS! It was all I needed to know. She also told her daughter that she would do the same for her. About 3 or 4 days after I had my sign, Rose's friend was taking her grandson to the Isle of Wight. She had a meeting there and afterwards they were sitting in the terminal waiting for the Hovercraft. Her Grandson who is about 3 years old at the time was playing in these potted trees in the terminal when suddenly he ran out clutching a big red feather and announced what he had found and that he would be giving it to Roses daughter. Her friend knew nothing of the request we had asked of Rose so dismissed it. After they got back they popped over to see her daughter and her grandson gave Roses daughter the feather.

I still find this sort of thing amazing, even after all these years. As a medium, something always happens to shock you to the power of the crew upstairs. They amaze me everyday. I still miss Rose. Rose was an amazing lady who helped me and never judged me. We were really close friends. I do feel her spirit sometimes and she still sends me Red Feathers.

I wasn't sure where I was going to head from Roses, but I would find a way with my help from upstairs. Again, lessons were being taught to me. I still had huge doubts about it all, still had the pain and loss from Canada inside, but it was a new dawning for me. The crew upstairs seemed to be pointing out so much to me and I was trying my very best to do what I thought was the right thing. There were possibilities and opportunities there. I felt like I had been given a second chance and just hoped I was intelligent enough not to waste it this time.

I think I had just come to terms with the fact that being a medium was what I was always going to be.

Chapter Ten

THE VALUE OF WEDGEWOOD

Portsmouth, July 2003

I HAD LEARNT so much from my experience in Canada.

As it turns out, it was the first of many lessons.

I had met the people that ran a spiritual centre in Portsmouth a few months before my first major venue in England. I had decided that I needed a base where people could come and see me. Rather than trying to do home readings and to advertise myself, I thought it a great idea to rent an office space. That way, they could do the advertising, take bookings, I could carry on with my job but work it in around my readings. Perfect!

I arrived at this centre and met the two owners who seemed very nice. They showed me the area that I would rent from them on a daily basis. I thought this a good idea, it had potential.

For some reason though, something niggled me about the whole thing.

It took a while to click onto this feeling. Then it dawned on me.

It still felt very impersonal – too much like business. Nevertheless, I saw it as a good way to get to help as many people as I could, as quickly as I could with the time I had available to me.

The charges to the customers were structured by the owners of the centre, but I didn't like what they had done. I thought they were charging people too much for my readings. Despite my foray into the unknown in Canada, I felt very uncomfortable, and still do about the financial side of what I do. I know a medium has to live but they wanted me to charge more than I felt was right.

What's happening Justin?

This doesn't feel right.

After the centre opened we did a few taster days for £5 a reading which was a huge amount less than they tried to charge originally.

I felt great doing these little sessions. I sat in a room on the top floor and the queue of people there to see me snaked up the winding staircase. I did several good connections and also several "OK" connections – but it was great experience and everyone went away happy, which was all I really wanted from the exercise.

I enjoyed myself at the centre at times, despite my inability to get comfortable with the atmosphere. After a while I asked if it would be ok to hold a meeting in the basement for several people to come along at once and for me to hold a group connection. They agreed to this and I set about getting people to come. Most of the staff knew people that would be willing to participate and we had around 20 people arrive. The whole evening turned out to be dominated by a lady and her mother. Their whole family turned up and took over an hour to get all the connections from her family through. It was an amazing experience for us all. The ladies enjoyed themselves very much. After the reading when everyone had gone home, I sat down with the owner for a drink and made a connection for her through to her father. She had no idea that he'd passed away as he hadn't been a part of her life for a longtime. She understood and confirmed everything that came through. Afterwards she asked me if I had ever thought of doing larger group venues. She mentioned that she could arrange a venue and suggested the Wedgewood Rooms in Southsea. I had only ever been there once to see a band as it was more of a music venue and they had never held a psychic medium before. I didn't really want to do the Wedgewood rooms as I wondered about my ability to do a show after my confidence had been so smashed in Canada.

We set about setting up the Venue and the lady set up a photo shoot and some newspaper and local TV interviews. I went along to do the TV interview and although nervous at first found it a lot of fun. It only went out to the local area but it was a success. The interviewer made me feel very much at ease. He had been given some details written by my new manager. The first question out was whether I had a lot of success on my recent US tour.

What US tour?

I had been to my sisters and done some personal readings for her friends but that was about it.

I couldn't believe it - They were lying to people to make me seem more experienced and important than I already was!

Bastards!

The rest of the interview went ok. In general, I was quite choked that I had done a TV interview, but I was not happy with my manager at all. I confronted her about the lie, explaining that it was something I wouldn't stand for and why was it done in the first place? She told me that it was just a small "white" lie simply to make me look good to everyone else.

It wasn't "white" it was practically "Black"!!!

After that, I wasn't sure how I would carry on. I was suspicious of them all, deciding pretty much there and then that it would not be a partnership after this coming event.

That's when it started to get worse! I heard (not from them I might add), that they were going to charge £10 per person in advance and then £12 on the door. This was way over any acceptable fee I was thinking of. Damn. I didn't want people to have to get a second mortgage just to see a Psychic….and a novice one at that!

I asked them not to and said that I would feel a lot more comfortable charging £6.50 per ticket as many people might not be able to come if they couldn't afford £10. They said that they would change the pricing for me before they sold any tickets. The tickets were made available and the money was to go through the tills of their centre. Another thing that made me suspicious. I was then told that no matter how many people came through the door I was not going to make any money as all the money would be spoken for in advertising and going towards the next venue. They asked me to take leaflets around Portsmouth and deliver them through the doors of the areas I had already done personal connections for over the years. My friends Claire, Vicky, Jamie and Jenna plus my wife went out in stifling summer heat to help deliver leaflets to houses. I wondered all along as to what my manager would be doing to help us out. They also told me that

I was to be billed as an alternative psychic i.e.: a taxi driver who could talk to the dead and that I was to keep it as normal as possible. This bit I thought was a great idea as this was and still is my main goal. To keep it all as normal as possible so anyone can relate to what mediums do and not think we are something special.

The night of the Wedgewood Rooms arrived and, with the memory of Canada crunching away in my mind, I waited in the wings to go on stage.

They told me the place sold out.

300 people had turned up.

This news amazed me.

Wow.

300.

My friends were all there and I was told by my best friend that they had all had to pay £12 as they hadn't already bought tickets. I asked my manager why she hadn't done what I asked and she said not to worry as I was worth more. I couldn't believe it.

Trying to choke back the anger, I paced in the little room behind the stage, vaguely aware of the music playing as everyone got seated and comfortable.

Worry about the manager later. Get this done

The lights went down and I walked onto the stage to a great round of applause from everyone.

What a rush!

The first proper venue in England and in my hometown too.

Just me, a chair, a beer, a pack of smokes and a baseball cap. More on beer in a moment.

I started off with a few jokes to clear the atmosphere. Not great jokes...a few one-liners and observations which went down well to break the proverbial ice.

This is it buddy!

I explained to the audience how I worked and what would happen, allowing myself to relax a little waiting for the first connections to occur.

The strange thing is that, I, my friends, family and even my manager did not foresee the problems that arose in a venue such as this.

The staff had kept the bar open.

Why is that a problem?

Well, It may not seem like a huge thing, but, during connections, people were walking up to the bar in front of me, clinking glasses, scraping seats, spilling drinks, annoying other people and distracting everyone in general - including myself.

On top of this, the bar staff were having loud conversations which everyone could hear.

I couldn't believe that all this was going on while I was trying to do my thing. It made it very difficult. During my "half-time" break, I chatted with a few people and they tried to get the bar shut until I had finished. The last thing I wanted was more noise and distraction on the next half. Well, the venue owners weren't about to close the bar and lose their profits, so that was that.

When I went on for the second half, the connections weren't flowing as much and I decided to stop for a while and asked if there were any questions. I was asked some pretty tough ones on various topics but mainly on what happens after death. I answered them to the best of my ability and the audience participation was great.

Then I found myself being heckled.

One drunken gentleman had apparently arrived with a whole group of people halfway through and they were friends of the staff. They all found what I did a little freaky and were probably there for free drinks from their mates. I was told they didn't believe a word of what I do. I understand that some people need convincing, but these people were just there to shout and weren't open to anything other than their own voices... This particular gentleman decided to argue with each comment I made, laughing with his friends and taking more swigs of his beer. I am pleased to say I held my own throughout the evening. He didn't get to me and I was polite and helpful despite his behaviour.

My friends were ready to pounce on the guy and throw him through the nearest window, but I took care of it with honesty and sincerity...my most valuable weapons.

What I would've given for a small bedside light! Or maybe some pepper spray?

I still appreciate a healthy level of skepticism always. As I think it helps to question thing in life and not to take everything at face value. Just be polite about it!

(Besides, it's not like I can say I have never acted badly after a few beers!)

I decided afterwards that it would be the last time I ever did anything that involved a manager. I would rather wait till the right time. Do it on my terms and in a way that would help the audience best. So another lesson learned. - Not to get ahead of myself, not put my trust in anyone other than spirit and not to rise to skeptics.

Just a quick addendum to this piece about beer.
Beer?
Yes beer.

I love a good pint. Don't get me wrong, I'm no lush and I certainly can go without it, but if you offered me a pint of orange juice or a cold one….well, go figure.

One thing I have learned however, is beer, and being a psychic, doesn't go well together. When I first started it was a great nerve-steadying device and a couple of drinks would be the Dutch courage I needed to prevent a mad dash to the bathroom to shout into the toilet bowl. But we are dealing with the sixth sense here. And as you know getting drunk dulls your senses, even your sixth sense, so you can fill in the rest of what happens when you have a couple more than you should before a large group.

.

I received some really nice e-mails afterwards – many about the connections I made and a lot that admired me for standing my ground when it got tough. I enjoyed doing the Wedgewood Rooms and in a way am glad that I did a tough one for my first outing. But I had learnt more valuable lessons from the experience.

I decided not to go back to that kind of venue and allow someone to dictate what I should or shouldn't charge people.

As far as what I should tell them about me as far as publicity and advertising goes….well, let the public make up their own mind about me.

I decided I would no longer need the services of my manager.

One of the most sensible things I have ever done.

The thoughts I were having had changed since my time in Canada. They were more positive, if a little doubtful….but it certainly was a start.

Is this going to work?
I don't know
I just have to trust in my guides more.

Chapter Eleven

FROM RELUCTANCE TO
ACCEPTANCE

AS YOU HAVE read throughout my life story, my main problem was acceptance of my ability. I just didn't want to be a medium. It wasn't a great career choice. I would have preferred to have driven trains or a porn star would have been nicer! Plus the schools careers office doesn't accept "I talk to dead people" as a viable thing to place on your CV. I think my main problem was that I didn't want to be seen as weird. I found that over the years keeping it real had been my main objective. I still don't understand what drove me to go from the living room to the stage. When I was a kid I enjoyed getting parts in plays. But they came with a script. You just had to remember your lines and everything would be fine. The worst part of accepting my ability was that I would have to prove it. I still ask myself why it has to be proved. Most of us believe in something after we pass away. So why then do we have to prove it.?

I guess I was always scared to upset people. I hated the thought that I couldn't produce. Also, I have always had a problem with being told what to do. I could never get my head around the process of spirit guiding me. They did need to be gentle, otherwise, I would just give up (and I had on several occasions) doing spiritual connections because I was told to do them by spirit. It also seemed that every time I tried to do home readings and then moved to group and theatre readings. I seemed to stumble. I always seemed to do well first part of the evening and then seemed to fall apart. I would then spend way too much time telling myself how crap I was. I would blame myself all the time, then as most human minds work, I would sit there and have to find someone else to blame. It was nearly always Spirit. I would sit and yell at them. I would also try and offer things to them, like; I will give up smoking if you come through just once more for this person or that. They don't work like that. It's not going to happen for everyone. But I wanted it too. I'm afraid that the "I wanted it to work this time or I'm not going to do it anymore" was something that came out of my mouth once too often. Like a spoilt child at the sweet counter. I want that or im going to hold my breath till I turn blue!! As you can imagine that worked!!!!!!!!

One day I decided that I needed to change the way I worked with upstairs.

After Canada things kind of got back to normal. I still wasn't sure of my ability. Then I did the show at the Wedgewood rooms. I still thought that the evening went really badly. It was getting to a point where all I could remember were the times that I stumbled. I would blame myself for being really crap at connections. It was becoming a hazard to the way I worked. What I didn't understand was how come so many readings went well. I mean these connections were great. Then some connections wouldn't hit the mark or mean anything at all. But for anyone to stand up in front of people without a script and to believe that something unseen was there and ready to give them information was an amazing feat in itself.

People have often told me that I must be very brave to stand up in front of people. They certainly couldn't. Then go on to speak to them without any form of prompting or script. How do you do it? My answer back then was

"Dunno" I'm not sure yet myself.

I think a lot of it at the time was that I obviously believed in something or why would I put myself up there. I did believe that I was talking to spirit. But in my naivety I thought that it was myself or spirit not able to make the connection. I would spend months beating myself up over what I was doing wrong.

I would shout at spirit. "How could you make me stand there looking like an idiot and expect me to still carry on.

I got my answer one day.

I went for a drive to Winchester Hill. It's a beauty spot just outside of Petersfield in Hampshire. It was around 3am and it was so cold. I had just bought a new car and thought that it would be nice to go up to the Hill and check out the stars. I stopped in the middle of a road that wasn't used much during the day let alone at night when it was really quiet. I stopped the car and turned the engine off. I put the car into neutral and put the handbrake on. I then opened my sunroof and turned off all the lights. I leaned back in my seat and looked up at the stars.

I was there for around half an hour when I shouted at spirit.

"Why don't you help me?"

"You want me to carry on being a medium you better help me or you can all F**K OFF."

Show me a sign as to where I am supposed to go. Surely I should stop being a medium. I wasn't exactly making any money out of it. What's in it for me? I called them a few names and sat indignantly in my seat feeling very sorry for myself. Then it happened.

The car decided it was going to roll forward about 50 feet. Well, I basically filled my pants. I could understand if the car was rolling back or forward down a hill. But this thing was rolling uphill!!! It came to a stop. Then I felt an amazing amount of energy. It was the same energy I feel when I get a connection. It's like being wrapped up in cotton wool. Then I saw him. It was my brother. I looked at him walk to the side of the car and look. I thought I was dreaming it. He bent down at stared at me through the window and then vanished. I thought that I was seeing things. I don't usually see spirit. If I do it's only in pictures in my head. But this was different. He looked right at me, like he was solid. He then disappeared.

I then got tonnes of information in my head all at once. It just knocked me for six.

Spirit was shouting back!!!!

First thing they said was "Exactly who do you think you are talking to us like that"

Then it all came through. They seemed to calm down a bit once they saw how scared I was. They told me that I was a very good connection to the spirit world. They didn't choose me for this work for the hell of it. They wouldn't have waited so long for me if they didn't want me to do this. They told me they had invested lots of time and energy in putting me in the right place at the right time. Both to learn how to do this and to learn my own lessons. If I didn't sort my head out and stop denying my ability to speak with them. They would shut me down.

I can tell you it wasn't very nice. Well and truly put in my place. I deserved that. But then something clicked. If I am denying my connection with spirit, why are they now having a shouting match with me? If they didn't exist then why would I be having this conversation? If I didn't have a strong connection with them they wouldn't be telling me off. I certainly wouldn't be listening.

After everything calmed down they then showed me a kind of movie. They showed me all the times that I had got a connection through. Then they showed me the affect it had on these people. The pain that they brought to the reading with them and then the relief they took away. They reminded me of all the times that I had been written too with letters of thanks and praise for my work. All the phone calls telling me how much better they felt. If I wasn't going to be a medium and spend the rest of my life doubting and denying then I had better stop right now. But they knew as well as I do now. I can't stop. I love it too much. It gives me such a sense of wellbeing and such a sense of love. I couldn't and wouldn't stop doing it. If it went a little bad sometimes, it wasn't me. It was just the information got stuck somewhere.

I was then reminded of a time that I went on tour. Ok, I didn't finance the tour. But I had to take nights off the taxi and lost money not working. My friend Steve had sorted it. He wanted to get my name out there. He wanted me to become well know. Also, if we made a little money back after costs then it's all good. The tour lasted ten dates. It was a flop attendance wise. In Cardiff 11 people turned up. In Swansea (which we drove 500 mile round trip for) 7 people showed. The best one was the one I did on my own. Steve couldn't make it to Weymouth and 4 people showed. I wondered why I was supposed to go on tour around the country and to lose a shed load of money and have hardly anyone turn up. I was told by spirit that it didn't matter how many people came. They all went away with the feeling that their own relatives and friends were safe and well. They were going to go back and tell people what an amazing experience it was. I was being reminded of the amazing connections I had done for these people. But I was also reminded of the people that just didn't understand their message. Spirit told me that I needed to learn something. Everything I get through is from spirit. Its not a case of something's are right and some are wrong, none of it is wrong. It's not me who isn't accepting the message it's them. It wasn't their fault or spirits or mine. It's my energy listening and feeling their energy from the other side. It's not going to be easy to get the message. Especially if people don't understand how it works. The amount of people who came up to me afterwards and said that they did know who I had through or they were either waiting for more information. Or they may have had to make a phone call or talk to their family about who it may be. They were then reminded that the spirit gave information that actually meant something. They had just forgotten. Some people didn't want to hear from the spirit. They had just come to make up numbers and sat there hoping that nothing came through. Or they were too scared to put their hand up and speak in front of people.

"Its not you"

Spirit then went on to say that they had watched me grow as a medium and had helped me grow. They had made sure that I could tell the difference between my own thoughts and what was being received from them.

So, I had to stop grumbling and get on with it. They then left me with one word that I now use all the time "TRUST" I have to trust in spirit. Trust in my ability to get the message across. Trust in the reasons they come through. If it's not being accepted then just carry on. Make sure that you go onto the next spirit coming through. If you do a connection where no one wants to accept any information then so be it. Please trust that we will get the information across. If someone doesn't accept it out loud. Then leave them with the information. You will then know that they will go away both accepting the connection and not wanting to say anything out loud or find out more about who came through.

They then told me about a book that I was going to write. It would be a book about my life and my reluctance to accept the feeling I was receiving. They also told me that the book would be a tool and manual for people who would be feeling the same way I did. I would become a teacher in this too. I would tell all my experiences through this book and it would help many people. I must admit the thought of a book scared me too. I was pretty good at English at school and when I was a kid I did enjoy the creative writing class we had. But I wasn't sure how it would come about. But I knew then that spirit would help me write it.

A few days later my friend Sue came to see me and we decided to go out for a walk. We took my two dogs to a place called Droxford. It has a church in the village and just beyond the church yard is a stream. The dogs were messing around in the water when I decided to tell Sue about what had happened to me. She then said "What about a book?" I nearly keeled over. I then told her that I was told to write a book about my experiences. She said it was an amazing idea. She would write the chapters lists and help me out. My friend Mark would then take over, which he did. But I had to write the book. I wasn't allowed to get someone to write it all for me. I had to give everything I had to writing it from the heart and spirit would help me. It had to be from me. Just me. As a receiver from upstairs.

The next day I was sitting at home and the phone rang. It was the local newspaper. They had seen a piece about me in the Welsh national paper and saw that I was from Portsmouth. They liked that fact that I was a taxi driver that talked to dead people. The interviewer came round to my house that afternoon and took some photos and did the story. I answered every question as honestly as I could and he went away. The following Thursday I opened the paper to see a full centre page spread about me. They had been really fair with me and not put down what I did. They were really amazing. I then went out and booked a new venue.

It went amazingly well. The connections were strong and fast. Then I got stuck. I had a young lad of about 19 come through. Spirit were guiding me to a couple at the back.

They didn't know who I was talking about.

"Fine". I think you do know who this is. I had given them so many pieces of information. You're just not thinking. I went on to explain how he passed and the names of his family and friends. They still didn't know. Not a problem. I then told them to go away and think about it and let me know. In the break the woman came up to me and said that they had just remembered the spirit and weren't expecting him to come through for them as he wasn't family. I told them it didn't matter and they were to accept anyone that came through. They agreed to try harder next time. I felt like a school teacher. The second half didn't go as well as the first but I got a few people to come forward. But what an experience.

It was the making of me. Those couple of weeks that changed me around. I didn't feel like crap anymore. I felt like I had truly embraced my ability and had taken what spirit had told me without reluctance. . I felt great. I knew that spirit were there. I just had to Trust in them. And I did.

At long last I was a medium

Chapter Twelve

I HAVE BEEN HIRED!

I WOULD NOW like to tell you that I had finally got over my reluctance to accept my ability and embraced my connection to spirit whole heartedly. It had taken a lot of soul searching and too much denial to get where I am today. Also, a lot of patience from my guides. I am surprised that they held out that long to be honest. It's like someone who is afraid of heights. I had to go over that high bridge to get to the other side. Even with its missing slats and only a thin rope to hold on too, I had to get over my fears of falling over the edge. But for years I was running around at the start of the bridge like a headless chicken, trying to convince myself that there was another way round. There wasn't. I knew it and so did spirit. So they held on in there until I was ready.

I have had a lot of amazing connections since I have accepted my life as a medium. They seem to have understood that I needed time to learn. I have since helped so many people come to terms with their loss and also helped lots of people come to terms with their own ability.

I have had lots of home readings in the last couple of years. I have been setting up several small tours of community centres and small halls around England and Wales. I have also had great successes on my trips to California. My friend Mark also started my web site (details at the back of the book!). I now have around two hundred e-mails a week from people seeking spiritual advice which I always find the time to answer personally. I have also been doing a lot of successful telephone readings which have helped people who can't make it to see me.

It has been quite a journey to where I am today. It has been a long road. But I have finally found what I want to do with the rest of my life.

Heal.

SECTION TWO:
The Manual

This next section is the "Manual" part of the book. It covers a lot of ways of discovering your own abilities. It also teaches about everything from meditation to how to deal with cynics in life. It's my guide to you.

The main theme of my work has been to "Take what you need". By this I mean that in life, try to take as much information as you can. But you only need to accept what is good for you. Everyone has their own opinions on how to access your potential. These are just some suggestions and also some ways that helped me build my confidence in the early days of realizing my ability.

Thank you

Chapter Thirteen

FULL CYCLE

FINDING A WAY to access your psychic ability is like any learning process. For some it's easy, for others it's like trying to run through a wall of porridge. Trying to connect with parts of your mind that you wouldn't normally pay much attention to requires a great deal of work, passion and time. First and foremost, it should at least be fun.

I find that if you make this learning experience into a kind of game for yourself, you'll reap the rewards a whole lot faster than pushing yourself unnecessarily.

Think of it as buying your first bike.

You've never been on one before, you know its going to take some time before you're King of the Streets. You have to learn how to stand on it properly first. Learn how to propel the thing forward without losing your balance. You'll fall off the damn thing the whole time, trying to pull off all the moves trying to impress your friends' .But the process is a hell of a lot of fun - even if you aren't BMX king just yet!

Of course, you are unlikely to fly off the pavement into a shop window by using psychic ability - come to think of it, don't buy a bike. Dangerous bloody things!

A fun way of checking your psychic ability is if you are walking down the street, driving or whatever… even just sitting in the park, try and guess what you will see next. I used to do this all the time and in fact still do just for the fun of it.

I remember doing an exercise once where I drove to work and said things to myself, testing my ability the whole time.

"The next car I see will be green." I said confidently.

I was waiting at a junction and the next car I saw was a green car. Then I thought I would make it a bit harder.

"The next car I see will be a blue Rover."

It was.

Then things got interesting.

I said to myself that the next thing would be a cyclist with a scarf on and a green light on the front of his bike. Sure enough, a cyclist went by with a scarf on - but no green light. Now, I was kind of pleased with myself, but annoyed that he didn't have a green light on the front.

Just then, around the corner came another bike. The guy had a scarf on and – da daaah! - A green light on the front of his bike.

Its fun, try it out.

It is advisable to keep a journal of your little psychic tests. Whenever you feel something that you feel is not your usual way of thinking, then write it down. Also, when someone calls you on the phone, and then try to guess who it may be on the phone before picking it up (without checking Caller ID)! If you're right, then write it down. Another one is to keep a dream journal beside your bed, so when you get up in the morning you can write down the dreams you can remember. This will help as some dreams are precognitive. They can also be from spirit guides giving you subconscious help while you sleep. It's all good for feedback. I have mentioned in this book that mediums need some kind of feedback from the people we have connected for. If everyone sat there and said nothing, then went away without you knowing if the connection was a success, then we would soon start to doubt the connections we are having. If anything strange or "psychic" happens to you, if you see a friend you haven't seen for a while and you were just thinking about them, then write it all down. It's a great feedback tool for you. It also helps you so you don't think you're going off your head. Also, it helped me remember certain readings and psychic things that have happened to me over the years. It's also advisable when you have done a connection for someone or a reading, and then ask them if they wouldn't mind putting their feedback in your book. It's always good to keep a record of the connections you have done. Whether they were positive or negative. It helps you with your feedback to go over the connections and there meanings. It may come in useful when you go to write your memoirs one day.

We are all born with a psychic ability and are able to connect with spirit. Over the years this ability seems to fade away for a lot of people. But, I think it hasn't, we just aren't looking out for the signs. Female intuition is a good example. It's referred to often, but rarely questioned.

When we have lost someone, most of us have had a dream about that person. They have felt so real. You could almost touch them and smell them, it's such an amazing feeling. To give a great example, when my last dog passed away, as always, I was heart broken. I have loved all my dogs without reserve. I have never gotten over any of their passing and I miss them very much. One night, I had a dream that I was in the woods with all the dogs that had been a part of my family from a kid upwards. They were all there running around, playing. I was throwing sticks for them and having a great time. My dog that had just passed came running out of the trees, ran over to me and I gave her a rub and pranced around with her like a complete softie I am with dogs. It was great. I could feel the heat of her tongue on my hand when she licked me. It was such an amazing feeling to be able to see her again. I cried when I woke up. I knew that it was her and all the others I had the privilege to know. They were happy - doing what they enjoyed the most. Their own personal heaven, running around in the woods chasing sticks.

These dreams are actual contact with spirit. I have heard some amazing stories from people of genuine spirit contact in dreams and then they ask me if I thought they might have made a connection???

Of course you have! And it's an amazing feeling.

There are some other exercises you can do. Ask for signs from spirit that they are there. I was driving along the motorway once on my way to Wales to do a demonstration. I was feeling a little low because we had done lots of venues with very little response. I know now it was all part of the learning process I had to go through.

I asked for a sign, something to tell me that I was being taken care of. All of a sudden a truck pulled onto the motorway from a service station in front of me. On the back of the truck was a huge sign naming the haulage company. They were called "Faith" transport.

There it was in huge black and white lettering. This may seem like a small thing to some, but to me it was the biggest thing since spreadable butter.

It's the little things that make a difference. Look out for these signs. I have some very good clairvoyant friends that wouldn't see a sign if it was thirty foot tall in bright neon words that said "SIGN" and hit them on the head – twice!

One evening, in my taxi I dropped off a fare in a place called Denmead. I was going through a hard time coming to terms with the fact that, as far as I was concerned, I was losing my ability and many connections didn't seem to be going the way I had wanted them too. I felt that I wasn't performing to my best ability. I decided to drive through the countryside on the way home instead of the motorway. When I started driving I looked up and asked for a sign.

Out of nowhere came an owl. It was beautiful. It swooped down and flew just above the windscreen for about three hundred yards or so. It followed the road and then perched itself on a telegraph pole. I pulled over and looked up at the owl, admiring its brilliance and majesty. On the radio came a song. That song repeated over and over again the same words - "have faith in us and we will get you on your feet again".

My Brother in Law, Brent, who is one of my best friends, lost his mother a couple of years ago to cancer. Before we met, he didn't believe in much other that what he could see and hear, touch and taste. It wasn't until he found out about my ability and saw it first hand that he went out of his way to learn more about what I did. Over the years he has learnt what to look out for and I think understanding the process has made it a lot easier for him to understand the signs his mother is sending him.

One morning, he decided to clean up the garage. He stuck a CD on his stereo and started shifting stuff around. He was going through the drawers of an old wooden desk that his mother used to own, and hidden underneath the desk was a secret drawer. He pulled it open and lots of pictures, of his mother with her friends, came out. Holiday snaps etc. And as he held them up, flicking through each one, the cd he was listening to started to jump. He listened to the line that was jumping and it sang over and over, "I had a great time" He understood this to be a sign from his mother that she was fine and she had enjoyed her life.

Look out for these signs be them small or large, in your face, signs. We all tend to wander around in the world, thinking we have a pretty good grip on things. Stop for a while everyday and look up. Think about why you are here. What it means to you.

As I mentioned earlier in the meditation chapter, go out for a drive or a walk in the middle of a clear night and look up at the stars. Feel yourself as part of this huge machine that is life. Its amazing what you can accomplish doing this.

Try it.

Lesson: Enjoy discovering your psychic abilities. Don't shy away from them and certainly don't be scared. We all have these abilities. Some are heightened in others. It's an amazing feeling when you find out what you are capable of.

Chapter Fourteen

MEDITATION OR PLAYSTATION

I HAVE READ a lot of books in my time on how to meditate and relax your mind for spirit connection. I have sat in group circles before in uncomfortable chairs being told, time and time again, that I'm not sitting correctly for the "positive energies" to come through. On the same occasions I have been asked to breathe in the light from an unseen, imagined golden ball of light in the air and blow out black smoke. You have to keep your eyes firmly closed in a blacked out room with whale song in the background.

Mmmmm!

I think there has been too much over the years of people telling you how to meditate and connect. If it works for that person, then great. But everyone is different. It used to make me feel really guilty for not sitting down for an hour or two everyday and listen to my breathing and trying to pull in energies that we sometimes can't feel. At the time I would rather have played video games and had a beer!

I say, whatever works for you. I am not going to tell you how to meditate in a certain way. I am not going to tell you that you should be seeing things in your mind.

We have different ways in which we meditate and the only way it can work is for you to do it your way. How you feel comfortable.

A friend of mine would go and meditate at the Holistic centre on a regular basis yet was constantly disappointed that the only outcome was that blue lights seemed to appear behind her closed eyes. It was explained to her that these blue lights are spirit and they are connecting with her. So seeing them week in week out helped her to come to terms with her own abilities. But she found out later that if she sat on her bed at night, listening to music with her eyes closed. The same things would happen.

So, in my opinion, you should relax and meditate in a way that works for you!!! There are no rules here. You could buy a hundred books on the subject and still find that lying on your bed, listening to music on headphones would be the only way for you to be comfortable. If that is the case then so be it...

I find the best way for me, and these are only suggestions, is to walk your dog in the woods. Find some woods in your local area, a field, a park, the beach or a lake is great. Take a walk. If you haven't got a dog then just walk by yourself (walking your cat or hamster is ill-advised and too stressful)!

While you are out walking, find a quiet spot where there is no one else around and just stand there. Use your senses. The idea of meditation is to clear your mind.

Hear the wind going through the trees or birds singing. Feel the breeze on your face. Watch the branches of trees sway.

At the beach, listen to the waves lapping against the shore and feel the sea air in your lungs while you watch the horizon.

At this point, it's easy for me to get all tree-huggy and hippy, but the fact of the matter is that in the hectic rat race we all scurry around in, we have forgotten to stop and take it all in. All the wonderful sights and sounds of nature and the beauty of this world are quashed by our debts, our twelve hour working days, and the need to look like Brad Pitt or Angelina Jolie!

Ignore the onslaught of insurance quotes, instant coffee and cable TV.

Drown in the sheer delights that nature has to offer.

Listen out for the thoughts in your head. Try to remember the things that go through your mind; they may be spirit messages...

Messages from spirit come through in different ways to all mediums. It's like this most of the time, for me anyway. Example: You are driving along the road, yet your mind is thinking of a conversation you may have had with someone or perhaps you are thinking "Did I leave the iron on?" or "Did I set the video?"

Well the voice you are hearing in your head is your own voice. You are still concentrating on driving or shopping or whatever you are doing, but that voice is there whilst you go about everyday stuff.

To confuse matters, for most, it's exactly the voice you hear when you are getting a connection. I know what you're thinking. How the hell am I supposed to separate these voices? Well, you just know. Go with it. Try it out. TRUST. You may fall over and stumble on the way. We all have. But the main thing is just try and separate the stuff that you are receiving from your normal thoughts. Try this; ask yourself a question and go with yes or no answers. The first thing that comes into your head, go with. Even if it seems out there. It's like the TV Show Catchphrase "Say what you see" Like flipping a coin to answer a question.

I used to think that other mediums were so much better than me and that they would tell me they can hear the voice of the person they are talking to. They probably can if that's the way they are supposed to get the information. But, if you are getting the information through via different means, then go with it. Don't expect the spirit to talk in their voice. Remember, they may not have a voice as we know it.

Their communication is done through the power of thought.

It may be a lot to take in, but the key is to "listen" and take in these thoughts. It's not about posture, breathing or strange music. It's about you.

Relax, let the world flow through you and listen to yourself.

You'll be amazed.

Lesson: You can do this in anyway that is comfortable to you. Listen to your own feelings on how you want to meditate.

Chapter Fifteen

COINCIDENCE?

WHILE WE ARE talking about your potential here, let's drop the word 'coincidence' from your vocabulary. It's not a word. It's an easy way for people to explain everything weird and strange that happens to them. As spiritual people we know that when something happens to us out of the ordinary. It's nothing to do with that coincidence word at all, its spirit. Your own blueprint that I have talked about. A little shove in the right direction from your guides. Nothing in life that happens by accident (another bad word) or is just a coincidence.

I think that the following stories knock the "coincidence" argument on the head!

My kid sister, Michelle was going through a bad time for a while in 1995. She had a boyfriend who was frankly, a total idiot! He didn't treat her very well and she knew it. Something told her she should leave him. She was also in a temporary agency job that she despised. She seemed to be going no where in her life. She was a trained nanny by trade. She had worked in many houses in the area for some very nice people. In the last place of employment she had worked with a baby and watched him grow up. Then he went off to school and she had to find different work. One Thursday, she bought our local paper "The News". It's had a job section in it once a week. As she leafed through it she noticed a job. It said "Nanny required to live and work in California" Local interview with previous nanny. Experience and qualifications required. She rang me and told me about the job. I said "Go for it". She was very nervous about the whole thing. She had never been anywhere abroad on her own before. She was also a nervous person anyway. Hated the thought of any interview, and starting a new job, terrified her.

She went for the interview and was immediately offered the job. Three weeks later with everything she owned in the world, we all said goodbye at Heathrow Airport. She looked so small and scared on her way through departures.

Around a year later she had settled in nicely. She was getting ready to come home. She had 3 months left on her contract. Then something amazing happened. Michelle had been invited to a BBQ that evening, but as her boss had meetings every Wednesday, she had to work late, so was unfortunately unable to go. . But her boss phoned later and told her she would be home early as the meeting had been cancelled. Michelle went to the BBQ with her friend. Half way through the evening two men arrived at the party. As one walked in he said hi to Michelle's friend as he knew her. The other one smiled at my sister. My sister then turned to her friend and said "That's the man I'm going to marry"!!! After chatting together for an hour. Brent then told Michelle that he wasn't going to come to this BBQ. But he was due to go to the grand opening of his friend's new bar in town. But the night before the bar had burned down in an accident. So, they had decided last minute to go to the BBQ instead.

Two years later they were married. They now live happily with their two children in California.

A lady e-mailed me once. She told me she had recently lost her friend and had found my website by chance! Whilst reading the e-mail, spirit were practically jumping up and down. They were telling me that I had to offer this lady a connection. I wrote back asking her where she lived. I get several hundred messages from people around the world. So I needed to know where she lived so that I could know whether to give her a telephone reading. She mailed back and told me she lived in Portsmouth, England. Well, as you already know, I live in Portsmouth too. I couldn't believe it. I decided to give her my telephone number for her to call me to arrange a one to one reading. She phoned the next day and was chatting away about arranging a reading and how she had found my web site by accident. I asked her where she lived. She gave me her address...It was two doors away from my house. She had no idea. She had only just moved into the house and we hadn't even had a chance to meet. I couldn't believe it. No wonder spirit had wanted me to do a connection for her. They had arranged it.

She came over that afternoon and we had an amazing connection which her friend came through with an unusual strength and put her mind at ease.

I travelled to America once on what the airline industry call a "buddy pass". This means that they allow employees of the airline free friends and family passes to anywhere in the world. All you have to do is make a small payment to cover taxes etc. A friend in California set up the pass for me to visit and do some more spirit connections. On the way out I had two stops on the way. I had to fly to Atlanta, Georgia, and then change to a flight to Salt lake City, Utah, then on to Sacramento, California, where my sister lives. A bonus of the passes was that I got to travel in First

Class. WOW!!!!! It was amazing. I had never flown first class before.

On the trip home I flew direct from Sacramento, California to Atlanta, Georgia. When I arrived at Atlanta I was informed that the buddy pass scheme was a standby basis only. They couldn't get me to London. It was Easter week and the only flights they had left were to Paris, France. Damn. I didn't know what to do. So I decided that I was better getting to Europe than waiting in America. I wasn't sure how long I would have to wait. So I thought at least I am on the right side of the Atlantic! I arrived in Paris and went to the Eurostar Terminal. I changed up the dollars from my readings that I had saved. It changed to 230 euros. I went to purchase my ticket and couldn't believe that it was 230 euros to London. I was a little upset at the huge price. But at least I had enough money.

When I arrived in London I went through customs at waterloo. I looked tired and irritable going through customs. Not a great way to look when you are going through the "Nothing to Declare" lane. A customs officer stopped me and asked to see inside my bags. Great, I though. All my dirty laundry all out over his desk. He asked where I had been and what I had been doing. I told him I was on a short break to America. I also told him that I was a psychic medium. He just looked at me shocked. He then went on to tell me that his grandmother had just passed over and he would love to know whether she was safe and ok. Well, you guessed it. I ended up sitting at his desk with all my laundry strewn over it getting his grandmother through. I needed that, I thought. It must be some sort of cosmic joke by spirit. I thought of them laughing their socks off at the situation they had put me in to do this reading for a customs officer

I arrived home on the Friday and because I was absolutely skint. I decided that I had to work on the Saturday. I joined the taxi rank at Portsmouth Harbour Station. After about an hour a group of 4 people came over to my taxi and asked me whether I could take them to Leeds in Yorkshire. I obviously jumped at the chance. The fare for that journey normally goes for about £400 in a cab. But I told them I would do it for them for the same price as a train ticket each. We worked it out at £300. After I had taken out my fuel costs it worked out, converted to around $400 dollars. So I got the money back that I had spent on the Eurostar train ticket to London.

Spirit works in the most amazing ways. Please never question why they put certain "road blocks" in your way. They are all meant to be. Just accept them.

Coincidence?

Yeah Right!

Chapter Sixteen

SEPARATING THE WHEAT FROM THE CHAFF

RECEIVING A MESSAGE has a lot to do with how the message from spirit is received by the medium and also by the sitter. As I have said before. It can be hard work getting the messages to people sometimes. Mostly it's due to not being able to get what the medium is seeing or feeling over to the person receiving the connection. Sometimes people just stare at you. But the worst kind is the one that won't accept a message from spirit unless you have given the dearly departed persons leg measurement or national insurance number. It doesn't work like that and it never will. The information we receive comes from spirit in the different forms. Now depending on what sort of receiver the medium is, depends on the way the message is given from Spirit. Some mediums see the spirit in a flash or hear the spirit in their head. It's mostly in the mediums own voice. You know that voice that talks when you think to yourself... But the information always comes through in a way that the medium can understand. In the mediums frame of reference.

The thing is some cynics ask why the message isn't given to us as a two way conversation. Like, the sitter asks the spirit questions and the answers get relayed like a phone line. It doesn't work like that, and I don't know why either. It would be amazing if it was like that. The way spirit gives its information, to me anyway, is in images and movies and songs etc. If I need a name for someone then they will show me a friend of mine with the same name. Or an actor or a film with the name in it Also, they will put song lyrics in my head or the year of the song I'm hearing has a meaning. Sometimes I will see photographs of the person I am connecting with. Other times I will receive numbers too. If I receive the number 61. It could have several different meanings. It could be that the spirit was 61 when they passed. They may have lived at number 61. Or they passed on the 6th January. Weird and hard I know. But that the way it is.

An example of how we get the message and give it is. I did a sitting for a group. I had a message for a gentleman. I had an image of the movie "Men in Black". Now if you have seen this film it has Tommy Lee Jones and Will Smith starring. So I heard the theme tune in my head and thought about what it could be. I went through all the scenarios in my head. Could it be the name Will or Smith or Tommy etc? So I thought I would just say what I was seeing. I said to the gentleman

"Who are the Men in Black?"

He laughed and told me he was a Funeral Director and there were three of them and they called each other "The Men in Black"

It's like learning a new language when we do this. Imagine that you are learning Spanish. Some people prefer a book course to read. Some people want it on tape or cd and others want to sit in class with a teacher or watch the TV and learn that way. Well, the information we get comes to us in different forms. If I see a rose I am probably connecting with someone called Rose or it's an anniversary? Either a birthday or the anniversary of the passing. They will show me sometimes the cover of Blondies Album, Parallel Lines. What that means to me is that there is a parallel between the sitter and the spirit. That could be either a name that the sitter has in her family is the same name passed down as the spirit. Also, If I see a movie with Tom Hanks in it, it will be that either the movies title has a meaning or the name Tom. Etc etc etc. Confused?

Yes it is confusing. The time you have to get this information processed is a matter of nanoseconds. That's why we cannot spend time analyzing the process or the stuff we get. It's in and out ASAP. It's a strange way of receiving information. It would be so much nicer if the spirit turned up, stood next to me in full view and then told me to repeat everything they are saying. That would make all mediums lives so much easier. But, and I never question this, it doesn't happen that way. The way we work is just it, WORK. We have to try hard understanding. Then it's down to the receiver in the audience or wherever to understand the stuff we are getting.

What we are dealing with is a living consciousness. It's essentially telepathy between Spirit and medium. Have you ever tried to mind read someone? It's impossible. But because a mediums conscious Spirit gets in sync with a Spirits consciousness. It's kind of like trying to talk to someone in a nightclub. First you have to get their attention from across the room. Then you have to shout loudly. If that can't be heard then you use hand signals. You can try pretty hard to get across what you try to say. Everyone will use different signals to say the same thing. Like if you want to know whether someone wants a drink and what they want to drink. You could come back with vodka and they wanted a brandy. It's still a drink but the message got confused somewhere along the line. So it's that way in what we do. You have to be able to accept the message as a sitter and not question why you're not getting the national insurance number. Some connections are very strong. Sometimes the spirit is able to give you so much information that you let it out and it's like talking to the spirit yourself. This happens every now and again. Its not that the spirit can't do it. It's just like anything in life. Some people are better at art than others or some are better at singing etc. Some spirits are better at communicating with a medium than others. Just as some mediums are better at understanding through practise. We are not using our voices or our minds. We are talking soul to soul. So it is like learning a new language but without the availability of tapes, books etc.

When you go for a connection you need to keep an open mind. We are talking to spirit and we want desperately to get someone through for you. Not because of our own satisfaction. We are aware that our friends and family and guides are with us. We are doing this for you to be aware of this too. Doing this job is like the TV program catchphrase. Say what you see. You have to help us with this. If we get something through for you, please accept it. Try not to wait for more information before you acknowledge them. They are working to come through for you. That's not to say that if I tell you I have your mother with me and she hasn't passed that I want you to accept it. Let me work for it. Just don't expect to get the person standing next to me with a megaphone shouting all the information through. It's like when you go abroad to a country where you don't know the language. Shouting in English isn't going to get your message across any easier. We have all been guilty of that. But as I have explained, we will try hard to get the message to you. Just bear with us.

Mediums also have what we know as "Ah Yes" messages. It's not until after the connection and everyone has gone home that people come up to us and say "That lady you were talking about earlier. Well I asked my mum and she said it was my Auntie. It's what is known as psychic amnesia. We all get it sometimes. We may not be able to remember our uncle Joe. But Joe is going to use this opportunity to come through regardless. You have to try and remember the information you get and then relay it to your family. I have been guilty of this once. A medium once asked me whether my mum had twins and one died. I said NO!! What an idiot I felt. How could I have forgotten that? I did correct myself straight away. But if you don't the medium may lose the connection.

Lesson: Not everyone is going to understand all of the information you put out there. It may be stuff that they will have to confirm. Make sure you ask the person to let you now if you were correct or not.

Chapter Seventeen

SOMETIMES EVEN WE CANT
GET THROUGH

ALL READINGS CAN sometimes go a little weird. It's amazing how many books only cover the best of readings or the truly memorable stuff and how amazing, the people thought, you were as a medium. Sometimes when you do a connection nothing happens. I have discovered lately that this happens to us all. I wanted to let you know about this. If you are a budding clairvoyant there is nothing worse than reading a book by a medium or watching a medium on TV and they do an amazing job of connecting the people with their loved ones and they get information on information and it all goes amazingly well. The reality of this is that it doesn't go well all the time. All of us from your local medium at a spiritualist church to your internationally recognised TV mediums have days or sometimes weeks where they don't seem to get anything right. It's part of what we do. We have all asked the same thing "what happened with that connection?" Why did that reading go so bad and the others went so well?. I have said many times after a couple of weeks of not getting much at all, I am going to give it all up and just be a taxi driver. I know the streets of Portsmouth like the back of my hand. I can have a laugh with my passengers or shout at them when they are being vile. Why should I make myself look like a complete idiot? Well, you have too. It's all part and parcel of being a medium. It's not going to go well every time.

Think of it this way. The best footballers in the country only get around 40% of shots at goal into the back of the net. It doesn't mean they're not any good at football. It's just that sometimes they don't get the shots set up properly. It's like that with mediumship. You may not be getting the strength from some spirit. Also, they may only pop in just to say hello before disappearing. Not every spirit can make it through with half an hour of information. They just want their friends/family to feel that they have come through.

Please don't let a few weeks of getting nothing get to you. It's not an exact science. It's a very hard thing to do. You are going into these peoples homes or you are standing up on stage with no script, just your blind faith in something unseen. You just have to realise (which takes ages) that they are there for you. Spirit exists and they want to come through. They want to speak to their relatives or friends here. But, some spirit won't come through for everyone. Not everyone will get a message from spirit. It would be amazing if they all did. Imagine the scenario everyone comes to you and all gets the most amazing connection. Apart from, of course, having two hundred people in the audience and two thousand of our other guests from upstairs. It would take more than a couple of hours I reckon. It would be nice though, I must admit. But for the most part spirit will only make the energy available to help those who truly need it. I'm afraid that your ego and your need to shine for everyone are not on their agenda. It's just a case of dealing with it and not letting it get to you at all. Otherwise, and trust me on this, there wouldn't be a single medium worth anything left. They would have all packed it in long ago for the easy life.

I have recently been talking to my friend Dawn in Canada. She has told me that she is taking a break from connections for a while. She did a connection for her friend. Her friend didn't have any clue as to what she was talking about or who she was talking to in spirit. After the connection she then ridiculed her for being weird and not gifted at all. It really hurt her. I know that a few years before, one bad reading would put me out of action for at least a month. I have been in this situation quite a few times.

One evening I went to a house in Wickham. It's a quiet little town just outside Fareham in Hampshire. I arrived at this ladies house and she showed me into her front room where Twelve of her family and friends awaited. After I made myself comfortable I started in with the connection. I explained the spirits I thought I had, then nothing. I then tried to connect in again with others, nothing! This went on for Two hours where I got so frustrated that I informed them I had had enough. I went to the kitchen and a lady followed me. Then an amazing thing happened. She told me that she wanted to speak to someone desperately. I tuned in again and her mother came through. The information flowed through for her. It turned out that it was the anniversary of her passing and everyone in the room had only wanted to hear from her and they had all known her. I did a nice quiet one to one reading and it finally went well. But when I got home I had forgotten about how well the one on one connection had gone and concentrated solely on the fact I hadn't got anything for twelve people. It put me out for around Three weeks. All I could do was tell myself how bad I was. I mean, if I can't get anyone through for twelve people. How do I get something through for one?

I also did a reading once for a group. The evening went really well. I took two at a time into the kitchen and sat with them. I seemed to get really great connections. After most of the people had finished a lady came in and asked for her reading. After around ten minutes I couldn't get anyone through. So I told her so.

We then went back into the main room with everyone and I took questions and answers and general feedback. The lady that I didn't get anything for then asked if she had to pay.

I confirmed that she did as it's a group payment of a set amount and it's only fair to share the cost with friends. She then said I was "Out of Order" and that I couldn't get anything through so I was "S**t" at being a medium.

Everyone told her to go home and then apologised to me. I would have taken that pretty badly at one point. But, I know now everyone is entitled to their opinion and she had the right to say hers.

You have to blow it off and think back at all the great connections you have done. Part of being a medium is being sensitive. But don't allow people like that to talk down to you. Explain to them calmly about the process. If that doesn't work then tell them to P**s Off!!!

Lesson: It will be hard carrying on sometimes. But please don't let a few bad connections put you off. Please try and think of the great connections you have done in the past. These will see you through the hard times.

Chapter Eighteen

A TASTE OF THEIR OWN MEDICINE.

I **WAS JUST** thinking the other day why do we mediums get all the hassle. If you think about it, take the professional sceptic, the ones that run magazines and go on TV as the so called sceptic side of the argument. They call themselves a professional sceptic. One in particular has offered $1 million to the first person that can prove life after death in a scientific environment. This has been offered to any medium that can prove that he or she is in direct contact with spirit. They think that we are all charlatans that pray on peoples emotions. Even on things like Living TV they have a disclaimer that says that TV programs like John Edward Crossing Over and the 6th Sense with Colin Fry are for entertainment only and differing opinion exist to the true nature of clairvoyance and clairaudience. Why is this? What isn't there to believe? Plus, how are the connections we give people classed as entertainment? It's so wrong. It's because of these so called sceptics. They are cynics in my mind. I think everyone should be slightly sceptical to begin with and not take anything at face value. But these people go out of their way to discredit what we do. Ok, check this. Would these professional sceptics and co like to go to the Catholic Church and offer them $1 million to prove the existence of God? Or just before Songs of Praise and the BBC every Sunday, a notice that says this is for entertainment only and there are differing opinions exist to the true nature of believing in God? You would never see it. So why do we have to be bundled under the banner of entertainment?

Go Figure.

Professional sceptics wouldn't dream of following the pope around telling the world that he is a fraud and his teachings are praying on the vulnerable. He has no proof that God exists? It's just a strong belief system that we all have. Mediums believe that we live on after our passing and that we are able to connect and contact our friends and relatives on this side. All the religions around the world believe in an afterlife and believe that they can speak to god in prayer. Why haven't the professionals gone after every religion? I say you should believe in what you want to. I have given my life to spirit contact... Just as a priest has given his life to something unseen. I think it's about time that the professional sceptic gets on his bike and starts opening his mind to the chance that this is the real deal. They should also remember that any medium who is in this for genuine contact wouldn't want their $1 million anyway. Believe it or not, we are not in this for the money. It means nothing to us. We do this for love and because we know how it feels to have lost someone close and received a genuine connection from a medium, one who has peoples feelings at heart. So they can stick their money where the sun doesn't shine. It just shows what drives them if they think that's what drives us. What we do is for real, not some joke. It's not fair they accuse us of praying on people emotions? What I find the most alarming is, every time they knock this process and tell everyone that will listen, that we are not in contact with their friends. They are taking someone's feelings about what an amazing thing they have just experienced and their own personal beliefs and squashed them

Its funny, I never thought these people could wind me up. But it makes you wonder what their agenda is. I have had some amazing connections and people have gone away feeling 2000% better. I just hope that the people who have had an amazing experience won't let what these people say get to them.

So, what was that about? Well, as you get working on your ability. You will find that there will be so many people out there ready to knock the wind out of your sails. They can do it too. I have had it nearly knocked out so many times. A bad reading or someone telling me that I am doing the devils work. Or tell you, that you are rubbish and nothing made sense. Well, you will get this along your road. Just please don't let this get to you. Trust in your guides. Take the negativity on the chin and remember what I have said all through this book. Listen to what you think you need to hear. But mostly listen.

Lesson: Don't take any rubbish from anyone wishing to force their opinions on you. You just trust in spirit and do your job to the best of your abilities. Part of having this ability is being sensitive. But you need to grow a thick skin when these people spout their views. By all means listen to them as everyone is entitled to their opinions and take what you need from their views. But if they are total cynics then walk away and don't think too long on what they have said. You will find yourself arguing your views with these people and never try to change their opinion.

Chapter Nineteen

MEETING MEDIUMS

IT WAS AROUND Christmas of 2003. I talked to
my friend Steve about doing some demonstrations
in venues around the country. I need him to help me
book these up and, well, pay for them as I was very
poor at the time. Steve had seen me work before and
liked what he saw. He agreed to book ten venues.
Hotel conference halls and small stage venues to
start. Steve also suggested that he wanted to go and
see a medium in action as he had only ever seen me
work. He wanted to see what sort of venues other
mediums used and what kind of turnout we could
expect, also how we were to advertise and also how
to get return bookings. We decided to go along and
see a medium, who I think is still one of the best,
Stephen Holbrook. He was doing a demonstration
in Swindon, so myself, my friend Sue, my wife Angie
and Steve drove there to see him. The evening was
held in a sports centre in the middle of a basketball
court. An odd location I thought. But hey, who am I

to say where to go. There were several seats setup in the middle of the court and the spectator seating was also used. We sat in the spectator seats and we settled down and watched the people arrive. I couldn't believe it when Colin Fry arrived in the audience too. Colin Fry has a very popular TV show called the 6th sense. Everyone flocked round Colin before it started. He gave autographs and settled down. I had seen Stephen work several times and always went away with not only a connection, but also the feeling of total hopelessness. This hopelessness stemmed from the fact that I always felt I could never be as good as these other mediums. I have now come to realize in the last few years that we all have essentially the same delivery system for the information. The only difference is the way the statements are made. Think of it as a version of the song My Way by Frank Sinatra. Hundreds of people have sung this song over the years. It is the same music and the same lyrics. But it will be delivered differently by different singers.

I was lucky enough to get to meet Colin Fry in the interval at the bar. He seemed very approachable. We had a great chat about working as a medium and the negative effects that professional skepticism has upon us. He is a very genuine, nice guy. I enjoyed meeting him. I also got to chat with Stephen again. He has really made the work of the medium so much easier. He has a way about him. It puts you totally at ease with him. Some people go to these venues and start off feeling scared and vulnerable. But Stephen puts their mind to rest and explains the process beautifully.

I have also learned a lot from meeting mediums, whether in person or through their books. My personal favourite is John Edward, the American host of Crossing Over. I have read his books many times. I always take something new from the pages, as I hope you will from this book. When I feel that I am rubbish at this, I always pick up his book and listen to him. He often says that when he had his own office space to do readings, he would have maybe ten readings a day. Some of them would go brilliantly. Some would go ok and others wouldn't happen at all. So when I feel that I am not doing well I take this into account that some of the best mediums in the world can't get it right all the time. I also seem to learn something new from these mediums every time I see them work or read their books. It seems that every year I do this work. I get better and more confident. But every now and then when I doubt my ability, I take inspiration from one of his outstanding books. They always seem to make me remember why I do this work. I feel as a medium I have grown up with these other mediums work.

Stephen Holbrook was the only medium to have got my brother Jason through. After the evening had ended I talked to him about my own experiences. He was very helpful. I will never forget what he wrote in my book that I had bought. He wrote "Reach for the Stars". Thank you Stephen and all the other mediums that have smoothed the pathway ahead for us all. Without the, frankly, brass balls of these pioneers putting their necks on the line and going out there on TV and on stage, it would have made the rest of our jobs very difficult. It has helped this work become so much more accepted. They take a lot of rubbish in their work everyday.

Lesson; Read, watch and learn from these people. They have been through all of this before you. Use their own experiences to make up your mind living with this ability.

Chapter Twenty

GOOD PSYCHIC, BAD PSYCHIC

I FEEL I must warn you that you have to be so very careful when selecting a medium to make a connection for you. Also, be very careful if you decide to visit a fortune teller to find out what's going to happen to you. We all need external validation sometimes. Even I have been to see mediums and the odd fortune teller to find out. As mediums we know that our friends and relatives in spirit are safe as we speak to them and acknowledge them everyday. We also know that whatever happens in the future is meant to be. But it's like booking a holiday. You have the confirmation letter in your hand with the receipt and your itinerary. But, you still find yourself calling the tour operator to find out if everything is going to schedule etc. Its outside validation from the people who know that will help you. That's why mediums go to see mediums every now and again. Not just to see how they work but to hopefully get a message. But, please be careful.

Let me tell you a story about being conned. I had just started taxi driving. I had been driving a cab in Portsmouth for about 3 weeks. I was working for a company that has closed down now called Mainline, Pompey, Strand. I was working one Tuesday night when I got a call on the radio asking me if I would like to go to Kent on a wait and return job. I was to drive a man to Sittingbourne for him to pick up a Greyhound Dog and bring him back with the dog. It had been quoted £200 which I jumped at the chance of earning. I collected the gentleman from the office and started to drive. There was a feeling I wasn't sure about with this one. I wasn't sure whether I could trust him or not. He seemed genuine enough and very nice. But I think that upstairs were warning me about him. Of course back then I wasn't sure of my connection and I wasn't going to turn down a job of that caliber because of an instinct.

We talked all the way to Kent. He had recently lost his wife to cancer and was raising his two daughters. He was a dog owner and racer. He said that he knew everyone in the office. He was also very close friends with a few taxi drivers. I didn't recognize the names, but I put that down to the fact I hadn't been driving for very long. We got to the destination about 3 hours later and he jumped out of the car and went round the back alley to this house. I waited for about 20 mins and he came back. He didn't have a dog with him. He then told me that we had to go back because he was around £70 short of the price and the vendor wasn't budging. He then asked me to drive him back to Portsmouth so he could get the money for the Vendor and some extra to pay me and come back a few days later. He was very annoyed that he couldn't take the dog away with him. I then suggested that rather than wait, I could lend him the £70 out of my bank until we got back and he could get the dog now rather than make the trip back up to Kent. He was very hesitant but decided that it was a great idea and thanked me. We drove to a bank and I withdrew the money. We drove back to the address and he got out and went back down the alley to the back of the house. I waited...

Well, you can guess what happened?

After about an hour I knocked on the door of the house and a gentleman answered in his dressing gown. I told him that I had dropped off a man; he said he knew nothing about it.

I wasn't sure how I reacted to this news but I can tell you foolish, naive and generally pathetic were up there in my top ten feelings at the time. Why did I trust this man and his lies and the way I had been duped. I felt very sorry for myself. I drove to a 24 hour garage and called the Police to inform them.

The officers arrived and the first thing they said was "Welcome to Kent"

Yeh, Funny!!!!!!!

They took a statement and informed me that I was not the first that had been ripped off by this con artist. I probably wouldn't be the last. He is apparently a heavy gambler who travels the country sometimes winning and paying the drivers but when he loses big he rips the drivers off with various stories of dealing in gold, Jewellery and of course greyhounds. The officer then asked me how I was to get home as I didn't have any diesel in the car and all my money had been given. It was my last £70 in the world till pay day and I hadn't earned anything that night. The Policeman then gave me £20 out of his own pocket. I want to thank that officer for his kindness. It helped renew my faith in people a little that night.

I did hear a few months later that the gentleman had been caught. He had gotten a taxi from a racetrack in Cardiff. He had tried to swindle to taxi driver out of a £200 plus the £400 fare. The taxi driver had apparently beaten the hell out of him and then called the police. I'm not sure of what happened to him. But, I believe in what goes around comes around.

This is a lesson really in who to trust. You may go and see a fortune teller, clairvoyant, medium or whatever. But please, before you do make sure you keep an open mind and a skeptical one to - but not a cynical mind. . Please take all the information you get and take what you want from it. Some people are deliberately out there claiming to be in contact with your friends and relatives but they are just trying to make a lot of money out of you at a time when you need help. You're all intelligent enough to separate the good from the bad.

I went to a psychic fayre once and listened to a palm reader tell a woman about her life and what was going to happen to her. I then over heard him say exactly, to the word, the same thing to another lady half hour later, then again to someone else. I have gone way beyond being shocked by some of the tactics some people use. Please don't think that we are all in this for personal gain. There are a lot of people out there that can do what I do. It's about making an informed choice. I and others will try our hardest to get the message through to you in the best way we know how, with compassion.

I think you should go and see a medium or psychic based on word of mouth and reputation. If a medium or psychic is doing their job properly then you will get to hear about them. A great way of finding a good psychic or medium is to wait before booking the sitting. Ask your friends who they would go and see. Basically allow spirit to decide for you. They will put the psychic or medium in your lap. Like the Phoenix Centre card I found in Tahoe. It will just happen. Go with it.

It's like when I decided to get a dog. I didn't want to buy one so I asked spirit for one. I asked them, if I meant to have a dog then please find a way of a dog getting to me. I waited a few weeks. A friend and fellow taxi driver was talking about his recent relationship breakup and asked if I knew anyone who wanted to take their dog from them as they couldn't look after him anymore. We got our dog. The second came the same way. I asked spirit for another dog. A few months later a man at my wife's work was given a puppy. He had never owned a dog before and it came as quite a shock all the work necessary. So he asked her if she would like another dog while they were talking one day.

So, wait for spirit to decide who you are to go and see. It will happen if it's meant to happen.

Also, I would like to warn you that no amount of visits to a medium will help some people. Please don't let your grief take over so much that you go and see twenty mediums to find out what you need to hear. I have done many readings and the people have gone away happy. But they have been waiting around for that one word or name or whatever, something that means a lot to them. I have got lots of other validations through. But they need that one thing for them to feel like their family, friend has come through to them. Until they get that they will carry on going to see mediums until one day, boom, they get their message. Then the grieving process starts. They feel they must go back to several other mediums to see if they too can get that person through. If they don't, it all starts over again. I too have been guilty of this at one time. Please grieve first. Go through what you need to do with friends and family and maybe councilors. But only after that, consult a medium if you feel you need too.

Lesson: Remember that spirit will bring people to you. Once you have a reputation for fairness and good connections, people will talk about you. It's the best way to get out there. If you're open and honest about what you are capable of. People will accept you for what you are.

I hope you got plenty of help from that section. I find that everyone is so different when it comes to the development of their own ability. It can happen for some people very quickly. For others it may take years. If you are meant to take this path, then it doesn't matter how long it takes. You may not get it straight away. But remember, it's not yours to try and get it done quicker. It's up to spirit. It's their timetable. They will use us all when the time is right. Some people get straight out there and get on with it with total ease. Others may find that they have to raise a family first. There are lots of mediums, psychics and healers that don't start their own development until they are retired. Don't lose faith or heart in this. It will happen when it's meant to be.

SECTION THREE:

Connections

This next section is the "connections" section. It covers some of the more memorable connections that I have done over the years. It also includes some connections that I have had to make while working in my taxi. These were all much unexpected as I have learned to close down whilst driving my cab. The last thing I need is for Granny to come through for the man in the back of the car whose blind drunk and covered in Chicken Kebab with Chilli sauce!!! But the spirits mentioned in the "Taxi Tales" part made their presence strongly felt. When this happens I certainly won't stop them. As these sorts of readings are really meant to happen.

Chapter Twenty One

TAXI TALES ONE

THREES COMPANY

SO THERE I am, sitting in my taxi outside the most popular nightclubs in the centre of Portsmouth. It was a Friday Night (my most lucrative night of the week) and I was doing okay. I seemed to making a reasonable amount of money. Enough to pay the bills cover my costs and, despite a few alcohol-fuelled scenes in the street from drunken revellers, I was having a good night.

On this particular occasion I considered myself lucky. It was a couple. I assumed they had both left a club called "Lush" after a good night out. The girl surprisingly got in the front seat of the taxi and closed the door, I thought I heard a rear door close and casually looked in the rear view mirror. The young man sat in the back of the cab. I found it strange, but assumed they were having an argument or something.

I clicked on the meter regardless, fare ticking away as I drove on, lost in my own thoughts as per usual.

As the journey unfurled, I decided to make conversation and asked if they had a good night. I asked the girl first and she said she had had a nice time out on the town. Out of courtesy I asked the guy in the back seat.

No response.

I asked again, looking in the rear view.

He had disappeared.

The girl in the front looked very strangely at me and politely asked who I was talking to. I was a little taken aback and confused, trying to explain that I had "thought" someone had got in with her.

In fact, I was almost sure of it!

She asked what he looked like and I explained as best as I could from what I had seen briefly in the mirror. To my surprise, as I went through what detail I could, she began to cry.

She told me that the person I was describing sounded like her brother.

It was a big moment for both of us. We had a connection - a bonding experience if you will........

and I thought it prudent to tell her I was a Psychic Medium.

We pulled up outside her home and an impromptu reading just literally occurred. There was no fanfare. No huge introduction. It just happened.

There were images coming through. Flashes of pictures, video and audio snippets raced in my brain like a VHS on fast forward. I could see the Prime Minister and his wife in my head. Without thinking I asked who Tony was. She seemed shocked at first. Then a jigsaw seemed to come together in her head.

Tony was her brother.

I was doing well.

I asked whether her name was Cherie and she confirmed that it was.

Another result.

I went on to explain that her brother was with her and that he had passed – somehow- on a main road, which was renowned for its heavy traffic and accident rate.

We spent about and hour talking together and she said that she had never experienced anything like what had happened she was very grateful and asked if her mum could visit with me. I left her my card and she walked away.

I never heard from her again.

About 2 years later I did a sitting for some people in Portsea. During the sitting the boy that had come with us in the cab had decided to show himself again and as it turned out his mother was in the room with us. I relayed the information being received from him and she confirmed that Tony was her son. It turned out that Cherie had misplaced my card and every time a taxi took her home she would ask the driver if they knew me. She couldn't remember my name and it was difficult to find me as most of the other taxi drivers had not been told about my ability due to my fear of some major practical jokes and rib-poking at my expense.

Chapter Twenty Two

MAPLE SYRUP

I DID QUITE a few readings in Canada. Some are worth mentioning here, though it's safe to say that however well it went, I was destined to have a high before I experienced a very deep low!

I did a reading for some friends of Natalie's sister.

We sat down and I was impressed with a man related to one of the guys there, Ben. He confirmed that his grandfather had passed away recently and that the information I gave him was correct. Half way through the reading a saw a monster truck with a towing arm on the back. I asked him if his grandfather had driven monster trucks. He didn't understand this and said no. I couldn't shake this image from my head so I asked him if his grandfather towed vehicles as a job. He said no and that he didn't understand this connection. After the reading he thanked me and left.

10 minutes later he arrived back at the apartment and informed us that he needed a ride home as his car had just been towed away!!!! His grandfather had been trying to warn us that this was happening the very minute we were connecting. The importance of this came to light when Ben went to the towing company to collect his car and found that – sure enough - it was taken away by a monster truck with a towing arm on the back.

I also did a connection for a girl named Dawn. I got her grandmother through and she confirmed all the details I gave. She became so moved by the experience that she left halfway through the evening and ran home to tell her family about the reading. Dawn became a very good friend of mine during my time in Canada. Helping me through the problems that I had in my relationship, I want to thank you Dawn so much. She has a way about her that is so wonderful. She sat with me one evening in front of the fire and told me about an ability she has had as a child. She could look at someone and tell them about their personality, likes and dislikes, their flaws and their good points. It was amazing listening to her as she had me off to a tee. Then she asked me if I could teach her to connect. I sat with her and we relaxed and she was instantly through to my friend Mark. She gave me all the information about his passing and told me what he was like and our friendship together.

It is amazing when someone like Dawn manages to get over her nerves and contacts someone for the first time. I miss being around Dawn, so much. She is a natural medium and will be one of the best in the world later in life.

One evening I sat watching TV with a man called Craig. We all lived in the same house. A large 7 bed roomed property in White Rock, British Columbia. I had never really spoken to Craig about what I did. He was a policeman and a very nice guy to talk to. I had a feeling halfway through the evening that his brother had passed tragically. He confirmed that he had and the reading went from there. It turned out that Craig and his brother were out sailing one cold day with 2 girlfriends when the boat capsized. There was not enough room on the boats keel for four people to hold on to. As the hours went by they took it in turns to hold on to the keel, but his brother had no strength to hold on. He turned to Craig and said that he it would be better for him to die as he was older than Craig and he had his whole life ahead of him. They argued for a while and then his brother slipped off and went under the water in front of Craig... Three of them were eventually picked up at sea and Craig said that he had never got over the guilt. I said that his brother wanted him to stop feeling so guilty and that he was fine now and watching over his life from heaven.

I find it amazing that connection can happen anywhere even when you least expect it. One evening I was in a bar in Canada when I saw a girl and her husband sitting opposite us. She was part of a group of people that Natalie had been invited to join through friends. I instantly got her mother through. I asked her whether she was ok and introduced myself to her and her husband. She asked me if I was the medium that she had heard so much about. I confirmed this and she asked in a funny way whether I had anything for her. I said that I did and shocked her when I mentioned that her mother had passed away. It turned out that her mother was sick and one day she got a little better and was released from hospital to go home for the day. She was very upset that she still had to go back to the hospital so she decided to go shopping. On her way home she crossed the road outside her house and was killed by a car. She came through and said that she didn't want to die in hospital of cancer but wanted a quick passing. She had asked upstairs to help her and then she was run over on her first day out of hospital. She confirmed all this and her mother said that she was happy she had the accident and passed so fast instead of being in pain for months.

I was not allowed to smoke in one apartment we lived in so I used to go downstairs outside the door and have a cigarette. One morning a man was fixing the intercom system. I had just finished a reading so was still very open to contact when all of a sudden a man came through to me. I thought to myself that it couldn't be for the guy mending the door entry system. But I got to chatting with him anyway. He heard my accent and asked how long I was in Canada for and what I was doing here. I explained that I was a medium and he asked what it was. I told him and he asked me whether I could feel anything around him, which you get a lot of when you tell people, and I then told him about his father. He was very happy once he had confirmed the details I gave and he told me that it was the anniversary of his fathers passing and that he had been on his mind. He thanked me for helping him and carried on with the door.

Chapter Twenty Three

AMERICAN ENGLISH

I LOVE DOING readings in the United States.

America has always been a love of mine, starting many years ago and I had always wanted to visit. For a long time I thought I would never get the chance but, luckily, I had many opportunities thrown my way over the last few years and have enjoyed every single moment spent there.

My Sister, bless her, ended up marrying a great American guy and moved out there – which meant even more holidays for me.

What a sister!

A few years back I took a "vacation" stateside to see Sis and did my first readings out there. She had some friends over and had proudly told them all that I was a psychic medium.

Another reason why I love going stateside is that I find the American people the most welcoming, friendly people in the world and very open to psychic phenomena. . I think that the popularity of John

Edward and similar well-known Psychics have helped awareness – many, many people have tuned into his show and others and there seems to be much more of a cultural acceptance and less cynicism in the states. The chance to do some readings for my sister's friends was an opportunity I leapt at with open arms.

They also have nicer doughnuts.

We had an informal reading in her lounge with just a few people. This went very well. A lady called Jill had a friend come through. She had passed away a long time ago. When I finished the reading, everyone stayed and had a chat. The people at the reading were very impressed. They said that they would tell all their friends about me.

I returned to America a few months later and the word had indeed got around about me. I found myself there for three weeks, averaging six readings a day.

It was an amazing response. It still amazes me the power of people talking.

Each time I return to the states, I find a bigger list of people wishing to meet me, all of whom are extremely open-minded and enthusiastic about what I do.

It's a great feeling. ….And, as I mentioned, they have nicer doughnuts.

I have had many memorable readings across the water, but I thought it would be a great idea to share some of the ones that stick in my mind the most.

Two ladies came to see me one afternoon. One was a friend of my sister and the other, an acquaintance, called Pam. She had tagged along for what she thought was a palm or tarot reading. Her friend knew that she would never come to see a medium as we "types" scared her and she was apparently a very logical and sceptical person.

She arrived; we were formally introduced and sat down. She asked – understandably - what I was going to do and I told her briefly how I approach my work. Once she realised I was a regular guy, she seemed to warm to the process slightly. It came as a great shock to her when her son, who had passed away of leukaemia a few years earlier at a very young age came through. I pointed out that he was still with her and the fact that she had kept his room the same. I also mentioned that she had a picture of him in her handbag and it was wrapped in a piece of his pyjamas with "Tigger" on it. She said that I was wrong. She didn't have this item in her purse. I persisted, asking her to look. At the very bottom of her purse, she found it. This all came as a huge surprise and, of course, it was an emotional experience for all of us. Afterwards she told me off for making her cry. She was a real estate agent and was showing people around a house an hour later – now she had smudged all her makeup.

Damn me and my make-up smudging abilities!

I did a reading one New Year's Eve at a party in our friend Mike's house in Lincoln, California. Mike had no idea what I did, but after my sister's husband had given him a brief explanation, he thought it would be fun to have some friends over, a few beers and see what I could do.

During the sitting I was talking to a man and I had his significant other through. I asked him why the name "Kelly" was important and he confirmed that his surname was indeed Kelly. After a short while I had a feeling that there had been an accident and someone's index finger on their left hand had been severed off. The man and his wife laughed out loud. And then he took his left hand out of his pocket and his left hand index finger was missing after an accident involving a saw at work.

I then went on to Mike. His father came through with lots of information – even to the point of mentioning nicknames. I mentioned to Mike that he had got up in the middle of the night three days before and he had been bouncing against the walls in his hall trying to get to the kitchen. He was having an asthma attack and had to get his inhalers out of the cupboard where he kept them His girlfriend a few days before had had a cleanup and had moved them from one cupboard to another. He was feeling around in the dark when suddenly behind the regular cupboard one of the other doors opened on its own. He walked over to it and he found his medication. His father had opened the door so he could find it. In the early hours of the morning, one night Mike had been asleep and was awoken to a noise in the corner of his bedroom. He looked up to see his father standing by a nightstand that he used to own and was now in Mike's bedroom. He saw him draw in the dust on it and Mike thought this was a dream when he awoke the next morning. When he got up, he walked over to the night stand and there was a message written that said I love you and also a smiling face.

I was invited over one day to some friends of my sisters to do a reading for the whole family. I was collected by a lady called Natasha and her sister in law who had flown in from Los Angeles to visit. Her grandfather was also there and they gave me a beer and had fed me an amazing lunch before hand. After the lunch I sat down and could not for the life of me get anyone through. I tried so hard as I felt that they had been so nice to me inviting me over. But nothing happened. I felt so guilty. I asked to be driven home after a few hours. On the drive home I suddenly got lots of spirit connections whilst sitting in the van. I got very confused though because I had a grandmother come through but she was showing me two grandmothers with the same name and also two sons with the same name. I asked them about this and they both said that they had grandmothers that had passed with the same names and they also both had brothers with the same name and problems in life. It was a very moving experience for Natasha and she nearly crashed the van on the way home. We must have looked a strange sight sitting by the side of the road in tears.

Chapter Twenty Four

TAXI TALES TWO

AFFAIRS OF THE HEART

ONE SATURDAY AFTERNOON I picked up a couple from the train station and began to drive them home. We were half way through the journey. The gentleman and his lady friend were chatting away as I drove through town. Quite suddenly, the chatting stopped and the lady started screaming at the top of her lungs. I stopped the taxi as quick as I could. Which as most of you are aware that when a taxi stops, its stops. Mostly winding anyone, up who happens to be following one. I turned to see what the commotion was in my cab.

The man was having a heart attack.

I jumped out, scrambling to get to the rear of the car and flung open the door. I had no idea what I was going to do yet, but I knew I had to do something.

I shouted out for someone to phone an ambulance and frantically checked for a pulse. He died before I had even got the car door open.

I had gone through a first aid course a few months prior and luckily was able to put this knowledge to good use. This was ironic seeing as the guy who ran the course had told us we would probably never ever get a chance to put our newly found skills into practise. Mmmmm!!!

I ripped open his shirt and saw a scar running along the length of his chest. It didn't fill me with confidence. Obviously he'd already had some trouble with his heart and he lay in front of me on the pavement.

A crowd of people had gathered around us and I asked if someone could breathe into his mouth whilst I did compressions on his chest. A kind man stood up to the challenge and we timed out efforts as best we could. It was a strange feeling. It felt like we were working on the resuscitation dummy at the centre.

Although the events taking place consumed our attention, I felt something else around me - something important.

I looked up to find that not only were there people watching me, but several spirits were intermingled with the crowd.

I don't know how I recognised them to be spirits but they were spurring me on - urging me to keep going until the ambulance arrived. I made the best effort I could, even though I thought it would be useless - my adrenalin pumping at full force.

The Ambulance arrived promptly and I helped to put him on a gurney. They got to work using those paddles you see on TV shows to get his heart started. They checked for a pulse and thanks to their efforts they found one. After loading him into the ambulance they took my details and the last ambulance driver gave me a quick hug

I couldn't help but cry like a total sap.

The emotion was too much.

I never did find out whether the gentleman survived or not, they must have got my details mixed up, but no matter - it is still the biggest most amazing thing I have ever done.

Chapter Twenty Five

CAROLINES HOUSE

MY FRIEND CAROLINE from work asked me to do a reading at her flat in Paulsgrove and I accepted. There were about 7 people there and I was asked to do one on one connections. I sat in Caroline's front room at a table and the people came through one by one. The first lady came in and asked me for a future reading. I told her that I didn't do those. She looked very disappointed. After sometime her father came through. He started with his details for her to confirm. She didn't seem very interested at all in what he was giving me as proof of him coming through. He then said to me very clearly that he was going to tell her a few things that were going to happen to her. He told me that she never listened to him when he was her dad here, so she had better bloody well listen now. He mentioned that her life was to take a dramatic course unless she changed her lifestyle dramatically. He had told her that she was to stop spending so much on her credit cards, especially in the run up to Christmas. There was also a warning that she would lose her job in a re- structure. He told me that she wasn't treating her partner at all well and he would be ready to leave around Christmas time and she was to have an unplanned pregnancy if she didn't sort her contraception out. I told her she could start by tearing up her credit cards and to make a deal with the companies. Also, to go home and be more attentive to her boyfriend, find a new job now, as it was the summer she had plenty of time before Christmas. And lastly to sort her contraception!

About a year later I got a phone call from the lady that had the reading asking me to come back. I sat down to do a reading and a heavily pregnant lady walked in and I immediately recognized her as the lady from the last summer. She then went on to explain that she had indeed spent a fortune towards Christmas time. She had lost her job and hadn't looked for another one. She was, as I could see, very pregnant and she was so poor now and having trouble with the credit card companies and her boyfriend had left her because she hadn't made any effort at changing her ways. I hate to be the one that had and I told you so t shirt on. But spirit is never wrong. If they intervene that much, LISTEN!

Now back to Caroline's house. An older lady then sat with me. I started to chat with her about what she could expect from me in a reading when all of a sudden a gentleman turned up and kept on talking about the old records in the loft and she wasn't to sell them. I gave her this information. She looked at me in complete shock. Her husband had passed recently and she had come to see me especially to find out about her husband. She had even asked spirit earlier that day for him to come through to me that night. She had indeed decided to sell all their old records that they enjoyed together and had bought over a space of around 40 years of marriage. They were in the loft and she had got them down before she was due to move to a smaller house. She had decided to sell them to make more room.

Another lady came in the room and sat in front of me with her arms crossed and just glared at me. I started to tell her what to expect from the connection. That she may not hear from the person she wants to hear from. She then interrupted me and told me that she was a very good medium and that I wouldn't be very good at my job if I didn't get her husband through. I just sat there completely shocked. What a thing to say to someone. I couldn't care less how good a medium she was. I will connect with anyone that comes through for her. She couldn't pick and choose. I was very close to kicking her arse out of the room. She was really annoying me off. I then felt someone's presence in the corner of the room but he wasn't coming forward. I asked for him to make himself known to me. I then heard him say that he didn't want to come forward as he had nothing to say to her. I then thought, sod it and told her that I had a gentleman in the corner of the room. I then described him from a picture he was showing in my head. Then I told her that he didn't want to speak to her. She got very angry and walked out of the room. She then proceeded to tell everyone in the other room that I was rubbish and a waste of time. Unbelievable! I wasn't even charging anyone at that time either. So it did annoy me rather a lot! I then felt Jason, my brother come through. He told me to carry on with the next lady in line and not get wound up by that lady. He then said, "Let's show her how it's really done".

The next lady to arrive was around my age so I felt

a little more settled. After a chat with her I then tried to start a connection. But I just couldn't seem to get my annoyance over the last reading out of my head. I stopped the reading and explained about the previous sitter. She listened to me rant for about 10 minutes about how annoyed I was at a so called medium telling me who I should be connecting with. In the middle of another spout about what she had said to the other ladies the same gentleman that stood in the corner came rushing forward and said hello to the sitter. I told her that he had come forward and that he was the same man who wouldn't come forward to the previous lady. I then told her some things about him and she confirmed this to be her father. I then asked her why he would have come through for the horrible woman before her. She flinched a little in her seat and then laughed. She then told me the reason. The last sitter was her Mum. And yes, she was a pain in the arse. I was so embarrassed. I made lot of apologies about calling her mum all those things. I think I swallowed plenty of humble pie. But she then went on to agree with what I was saying. Her mum was a medium and fortune teller. She had told her mum that she felt she had the ability. Her mum had then told her that she didn't and that she was the only medium in the family. She then told me that she intended to go back to her mum and everyone else and tell them what an amazing medium I was.

A few days later I got a letter from the daughter to explain that she had gone back into the room with all the other people. They were all talking about how amazing I was. Her mum had told her that I was rubbish and wasn't a medium like her at all. She said that she disagreed with her and told her that her father had come through for her and said that he didn't want to talk to his wife at all. This made everyone who knew her laugh. It also helped her come to terms with the fact that she can finally after all these years disagree with what her mum says. She found the courage to argue with her mums views.

Chapter Twenty Six

TAXI TALES THREE

BABY BOOM

ONE EVENING, WHILST working at the Guildhall in Portsmouth, I sat on the rank in my cab and a doorman came over from the club opposite. He wanted a lift home after a long shift and got in the front seat. I knew him as we had said hello on quite a few occasions before.

On the way home he asked if it was true that I was a medium. I confirmed this with him. He laughed and said that he didn't believe in much of that c**p (as he put it). He then asked me to tell him about some of the readings I had done. After telling him about some of the connections I had done recently, he then informed me that I was talking s**t. I wasn't about to argue with a 6'5" man built like an outdoor privy. But after a while I thought, no way, He is an ordinary man and I'm up for a challenge. I decided to connect to spirit when we stopped outside his house. A small man came through and told me he was his grandfather and that he had passed away around a year before. He also informed me that the doorman's girlfriend was currently pregnant and she was expecting a girl. He had also recently been to his grandfather's grave as it had just been the anniversary of his grandfathers passing.

I gave him the information I was receiving wincing! He just sat in the taxi and stared at me. I honestly thought he was going to either run away or punch my lights out. But, to my surprise he just burst into tears. He confirmed that his grandfather had passed. He had just been to the grave a couple of days before. His girlfriend was pregnant and they were hoping for a girl. It was quite strange to see a huge man in his line of tough work crying in the front of my taxi. But it was also an amazing experience for both of us.

He has now told me after several conversations that he was always a firm believer in the after life. He was hoping that he got a message from me and had actually made a point of getting in my taxi that night. He had hoped that his grandfather would come through. He told me that he felt he needed to keep up the hard man persona just to test me and my ability.

A few months later his girlfriend had the baby girl that he wanted.

That same night I got a call on my mobile. It was from a friend of mine. He wanted to be picked up from Gunwharf Quays in Portsmouth. Gunwharf is a brand new shopping centre with bars and clubs that had just opened in Portsmouth.

My friend had been out for a meal with his wife and in-laws. I collected them all and took his in-laws home first. We then started to drive to his home in Waterlooville which is about 8 miles outside of Portsmouth. On the way back his wife was asking me about how my connections were coming along and whether or not I wouldn't mind coming around to her house one day to do a reading for her family. I had no problems with this as I will read anyone that asked nicely.

After a couple of miles I was interrupted by spirit. I tried to shake it off because sometimes it can be very difficult concentrating on driving and trying to understand the images I am receiving from the crew upstairs. But this one was a strong one. So I waited until we got to their house. I then informed her that I had someone with me. I couldn't tell her who it was as they weren't giving me any information like that. I thought it was a little odd as it's usually someone that wants to confirm to their family or friends that they are ok. All I heard from this one was that my friend's wife was pregnant.

I then went on to tell her this. She said that they hadn't been trying for a baby, although they did want one. They had a 2 year old boy already and another child had been talked about but not planned. My friend, who still thinks what I do is way too weird, informed me of the fact that I was freaky and gave me a look that I have received from him many times over. I then wished them goodnight and left to go back to the Saturday nights work.

About two months later I picked up my friends from Gunwharf. One of my friends then told my other friend to tell me his news. I asked him what he needed to tell me. He said I was freaky and weird and gave me that look again. I asked him what was going on.

His wife was pregnant.

Chapter Twenty Seven

THE CATS WHISKERS

I DID A reading in Wales for a lady called Lynn.

Her husband had passed. I had previously done
a reading for Lynn's niece who lived in a place called
Whitely near Fareham, Hants. At the time, her uncle
Keith had come through. The connection was very
strong and she was able to confirm everything that had
been said without question or need for clarification (I
love reading like that)!

As it turned out, I was going to be visiting my Dad
in Whitland, Carmarthenshire, and the following
week she wondered if it was possible for me to get in
contact with her Aunt and do a private sitting for her
- she lived a few miles away from my dad in Tenby.

Of course, it was no problem and I drove over one
evening where she met me outside her home. It was a
beautiful large house that would at one time have been
a hotel right on the seafront. She had a warm smile

and welcomed me like we had known each other for many years.

I liked her immediately - a wonderful woman with a great heart. She had lost her husband recently and, even with the bubbly persona, I could see and feel the strain she was under. It was as if she was just going through the motions.

We decided that it would be an excellent idea to go to her husband's club, where they used to socialize together with all their friends, to do the reading. I was introduced to many of them and we settled down at the bar for a chat.

I was immediately impressed by an image of her husband. He came through quite strong from the outset and talked about his time with her, how he passed and that he was greatly missed by his beloved wife. I asked her whether or not she had some kind of financial problem linked with his passing. She confirmed that he had changed credit cards just before his sudden, unexpected passing. The credit card that he had moved to didn't have insurance attached to it, so in the unlikely event of his death the card would still have to be paid in full. He confirmed all this to me and passed to Lynn that everything would be okay with this debt and that he was sorting it out. She asked how, but he wouldn't say anymore on the subject. He also pointed out that one of the cats had gone missing and that he was to be found in the back of a shed in an alley really close to the house. She confirmed this in amazement and went on to explain that they had looked everywhere for this cat and it had been at least two weeks since he was last seen.

Once the connection had been completed, she thanked me and asked me to keep in touch.

A few weeks later she phoned me at home in a state of shock. She said that they had indeed found the cat. He was a little worse for the wear. But okay. He had indeed been hiding out in a shed at the end on an alleyway. He had been there for a few weeks and was starving.

She also told me that balance on the credit card her husband had mentioned was roughly two thousand pounds and of course she had been very worried that she couldn't afford to pay it. A few days after I left Wales she had a phone call from an insurance company looking for her husband. He had a strange surname and they had been trying to track him down. He had a small insurance policy with them and that it was to pay out at that time - it was worth exactly £2000.

She was just amazed and shocked as one might expect. I pointed out that spirit know all these things and in most cases will make good on there promises. They are never wrong and they should be fully trusted in these matters. The power of spirit sometimes still shocks even me.

And the cat was okay

Chapter Twenty Eight

TAXI TALES FOUR

WHERE WRENS DARE

ONE SATURDAY I was working in the town centre and four lovely ladies got into my taxi. They were all in the Royal Navy; they were on shore leave and were looking to go out on the town so we headed off to the nightclub area in Southsea.

On the journey I had a feeling of sadness around one of the girls and was immediately impressed with a picture of her mother.

We got to the centre of town and the conversation in the back went around to the fact that there was a medium doing a show at the Wedgewood rooms.

"He's a taxi driver. Do you know him?" One of the girls asked.

"Um ...Yes," I replied, "You could say that!"

After explaining that it was me, they asked me if I could do them a personal reading. I agreed to this, but asked if they would like to come to the show.

Unfortunately, they were on deployment on that night and couldn't come.

As they got out, I gave them a card with my telephone number on. I turned to the last girl emerging from the back seat, Sonya. I mentioned that her mother was with her. She started to cry and we chatted for a short time whilst she confirmed the details that I gave her. The girls were very pleased - I would do a personal reading for them and they would call at the end of their deployment when all the girls would be free.

About 6 months went by and I hadn't heard from them, forgetting the whole incident. One Saturday night I Passed the Naval base and decided to go to the taxi rank in Edinburgh Road. I never normally use that rank as it was a busy night and I would normally used the Guildhall where the action was. For some reason, I took a last minute turn and drove to this rank instead.

Four girls got in and I asked where they were going. Then one of them gasped very audibly, to the point where I assumed she sat on a feather. She asked if I was Justin. It was the Navy "Wrens" I had picked up six months ago and that they had been out all day and over lunch had all decided that it was now time to call me for a personal reading.

We worked out the details and it was booked.

I went round to sit for 8 people and Sonya's mother came through straight away and gave her lots of information to confirm this. She had passed away earlier that year of cancer and Sonya had taken on the role of mother to her niece and had been very brave. She confirmed all this information and I went on to do a few more readings. At the end of the last reading I asked her if she wouldn't mind talking to me privately as I had some information for her to confirm that her mother was still around her that may embarrass her. She told me that she didn't get embarrassed easily and I could tell everyone. Well her mother then went on to say that she knew about the Rampant Rabbits!!!!! I knew this was a massage device of a – shall we say - private nature. Eight red faces later and Sonya explained that they had shown the said "device" to their friend about an hour before I arrived as her friend wanted one after splitting from her boyfriend.

I'm not sure who was more embarrassed - them or me. Sonya's mum had been there at the time and had seen them messing around.

Sonya and I are now very close friends and I would like to thank her for being brave enough to let me tell this story.

I know I wouldn't!

Chapter Twenty Nine

COLIN

I FIRST MET Colin at a friend's house. I was called by my mother and asked if I would go round to her friends house a do a reading for her and her family. I agreed as anything for mum. If I didn't do anything for her she would get the hump. And you never ever want to do that to my mum, trust me! I arrived at her friend's house and immediately felt a really heavy weight on my shoulders. I just didn't feel right. She had a lovely home and I have met her a few times. She is one of the funniest people I have met. She is always laughing and joking. When I went into the kitchen she greeted me with a huge smile and thanked me for coming. I had a chat with her about her family and friends and had a laugh with her and her daughter. We went into the living room with a beer and carried on chatting. She managed to clear the air a little but I still felt really uncomfortable. Then the reason I felt bad walked into the room. There was an instant drop in temperature with this gentleman. I just felt like crying. It was an energy that just smelt of loss, horrendously of despair. I noticed as well that a young girl walked into the room behind him. I could feel her sit down next to him and put her hand on his shoulder. She then smiled at me and I asked him whether he knew this girl.

Colin had lost his daughter a few months before to Meningitis. She was 13 years old and called Lizzie. She had got home from school on the Friday with a bad headache. She passed away on Sunday. I just felt total despair for this man. I suppose I felt angry at spirit for the first time. I have never blamed upstairs for anything about taking people over to spirit before. But found myself really annoyed for this man. His daughter was his best friend and all he had since the break-up of his marriage from her mother. They spent lots of time together with his son too and they had bonded so well. (Unlike a lot of teenage daughters and fathers). It just seemed so unfair. I did the connection and got a lot of validation from him. She came through with things like the fact that she would borrow his socks with the England flag on the side. She would return them a few days later smelling really bad. His mood lightened a little whilst remembering that she had really badly smelling feet. She also brought up lots of information about what signs she was showing the rest of the family that had gathered. She pointed out to her young cousin, Casey that she had a photograph of them both together. She pointed out the date on the side of the photo. All the information was confirmed. This was a very strong connection and also a much needed one.

She then smiled and left the room. I looked over at Colin and he was smiling. The whole atmosphere in the room had lifted. It was at that point that I realised that the happiness was from Lizzie in spirit because she had an understanding, like all spirit does, about the reasons they have to go. The despair was from Colin as to why she had to be taken.

Colin once told me that before Lizzie had passed over to spirit, he was a very selfish person. Who, like most of us here, based his life on what he could achieve financially and materialistically. He told me that he was driving home a couple of weeks after our reading and saw a man in a new Mercedes soft top. He had a new suit, sunglasses, and was talking on his mobile phone and looking around him for people to look at him to see what he had achieved. Colin said that he looked at the man and realised that all of it meant nothing. His daughter was gone and where once he had wanted the things he saw in the man in the Mercedes, now all he wanted was his daughter back. It meant nothing to him anymore.

I have spoken to lots of people who have been like Colin before they have lost someone. I think it does put life's wants and needs into perspective. Why do we insist on chasing the 'all mighty dollar' for things that we feel we need? Why do we need a huge house in the country and lots of smart expensive cars? As long as we have family and friends and most of all love, then that is all we need to get by. Without the love of my family, I would have lost it years ago. They have helped me in so many different ways over the years that I can't count all the love they have dished out.

Colin has now found out after my reading and several others by some great mediums that he too has ability for spirit contact. He has decided that when the time is right he will learn how to heal people. He has told me that he wishes to help fathers who have lost children to come to terms with their own personal pain. I know he will do well at this. Lizzie has told me that this is what he has to do. She has also told Colin that her passing will not cause pain, but will affect healing for so many others.

Colin and I are now firm friends. We help each other. We once went for a drive at 3am. Just for a chat. We went to Rowland's Castle in Hampshire which is right out in the countryside. As we drove we talked about death of the body and what happens to us and where we go. We talked about seeing and understanding signs received. There was a full moon. I stopped the car and we were just amazed as in front of us 30 or 40 deer ran across the road. Colin looked at me and said, "That's a message from Lizzie". She is happy and safe. Is that what it's like in Heaven?

You know, I think it is.

SECTION FOUR
Questions and Answers

This last section is my interpretation of questions I receive both from audiences and e-mails.

During my meetings where I demonstrate my ability, I cover lots of aspects of spirit connection and what happens to us when we pass over. Both through the explanation of the process and also my own philosophy of how the process works. It's mostly a few things I have picked up over the years. Both from spirit and books I have read. They have taught me a great deal about what happens when you pass over and why we exist at all. Also, why life is so hard and what we have to gain from it.

I hope you gain a little more knowledge from these answers to help you understand a little more about how this all works.

What happens when we pass over?

AT THE MOMENT of body death, the spirit removes itself out of the body. It is still attached to the body through the chest area with a silver cord. The sprit then snaps the cord and is met by a bright light. Sometimes the spirit will hang around the room. In the case of near death experience, of course it is still attached as the cord hasn't been broken yet. The spirit will then watch over its body. The spirit will, after an undetermined time be told by their guides that it's not time and will wait and watch until the body is brought back to life and at that point the spirit then re-enters . The moment we pass we release from our bodies and go on a kind of train journey. We leave behind on one platform, all the people we have known in this life and then when we get to the platform on the other side, and we are met by people who have passed on before us. When we are ready we are shown a kind of movie based on what we have achieved in this lifetime, also what we have done good and bad. The bad is not judged but we feel how the people that we wronged felt. It supposed to be a pretty horrible thing to experience our negativity towards people and our negative actions. We feel everything through every part of our soul. If you have done nothing but spread love and happiness through this life, then you feel that love and appreciation. But if you have been a negative person. I.e. racist, sexist etc you feel how those people felt about you and the hurt you caused. None of us are Angels on Earth but we can do a lot to condition our minds and souls into not being negative. Next time you feel negativity towards someone, maybe because of their race or sexual orientation or just that they seem less educated than you or even odd in some way, please remember that any of those thoughts are felt by you when you pass. These people have feelings. They are spirit just like you. They have the same type of blood as you do. Their feelings can be hurt just as much as yours can by your actions.

Who are your guides?

YOUR GUIDES ARE spirits that have chosen to work with you during your life here... Some have lived here with you or with others before. Some have never lived on the earth plane. Someone once asked me why the top guides are usually Red Indians or monks etc. It does take a long time to become versed in life and I have been told it's a wonderful experience being a guide. I think that it takes a long time to learn from various lifetimes to be able to help others in their life.

Your guides can be anyone from any walk of life. You have any amount of guidance from experts versed in any field of expertise for any type of problem you may encounter during your lifetime. You have your main guides who will be higher being on a different level of consciousness to the other guides. I think it's kind of like the yellow pages in a way. (Not belittling it or your intelligence here!). If you need a plumber for a job in your bathroom you would pick up the yellow pages and call a plumbing company. The Head Office of the plumbing company then would call a plumber from their company that would then come round and sort out your leak. Well, guides are the same. When you need a decision to be made then the higher guides "head office", I like to call them, contact the lower guides and they then come to your aid. They may be in your life for a few seconds to steer you on the right course. Or they may need to stay for a while longer maybe to help you meet someone that will become your partner in life. Or some will be with you from the day you're born to make sure that you're towing the line. In Some lives, the guides never get any acknowledgement from the spirit within you. Some people just don't believe or are not open to the process of spirituality enough to realise that they have any guidance at all. Although how many times have you heard someone say, after an accident that they were being looked after on that day? Well, they were. I have heard stories of having the most horrific accidents and not even bruising themselves. I am sure that they have had forewarning of some kind that they were going to

have an accident and their guides have almost, broken their fall. I had a motorcycle accident in September 1992 where I broke my leg. I should have died that day by rights. I have hit the car in front so hard and my head hit the back of the boot. I flew back 30 feet and landed in a heap. I should have died. But, I believe that my guides, Jason and Mark were there to help me.

What is Fate?

BEFORE YOU ARRIVE from spirit you set out a blueprint for your life. You have lessons to learn in this lifetime and have a connection with your guides through it. Kind of like a GPS tracking system. You set the destination and the places you want to visit in between. You set the course and the computer then tells you which way to go the easiest and quickest route. But as with anything, sometimes human will takes over and you deviate from the blue print. Guides then step in as the computer does and sends you right back where you should have turned. That's why sometimes you make a decision and go for it. And after a couple of months you may regret that decision or feel like you are taking one step forward and two steps back. The two steps back are your guides putting you back where you started from. So if you feel that you're starting over again all the time. Enjoy it. Take it all on the chin because it's the guide's way of putting you back on track. You may not like the track that you're on. But YOU chose it and it's always seems to work out in the end.

What happens when someone dies tragically?

NO MATTER HOW tragically someone passes, it is part of that spirits own destiny because of a kind of blueprint they have made before they arrive here from spirit. You work out yourself that you will pass on a certain day at a certain time and in what circumstances the spirit has chosen, and also when you hope that you have learned all the lessons you need to. Because your spirit is aware of that time. If you were to pass over in a car wreck, the spirit jumps from the wreck just before the wreck happens. Your body is then without spirit and can not feel any pain. Once you reach the other side, sometimes it is still a shock to the system and I believe that you are looked after and helped with the transition.

What happens when someone dies after a long illness?

THE PAIN IS gone. When someone is very ill their spirit leaves their body periodically getting ready for the time when it will finally go. I believe they feel no pain and that they have seen what lies ahead of them and the spirit can start healing from within the body inside while the body is deteriorating. It's a very hard thing to witness this for anyone here. We have each individually decided on the way we are to pass over and what we need to learn from each life and death of that life. It's so very hard for people here to understand why some people need to suffer so much. But I believe its all part of some Karmic master plan. It's hard to not want to help that person cross over and end their suffering here. But this is something that must never happen. It's all part of the universal plan. I don't personally understand it as you won't until you eventually pass over. I have been told that if ever you become seriously ill, you have to let it run its course for whatever reasons you set out before arriving here.

Do we come back?

YES, MANY TIMES over.

Think of our bodies as a car. When it's born it's all shiny and new. You drive around in it feeling very proud of it for a few years. Then as the years go by you tend to take it for granted a bit. Some people will maybe crash it a couple of times and some will write it off. Others may check the oil occasionally. After a while the car gets old and you are driving it around things are going wrong and its falling apart at the seams. You decide it's on its last legs and you scrap it. When you get out of that car - you're the same!!!! You're the same driver as when you first drove it, just little wiser. Well that's the soul, the driver is the soul and your body is the car. Your soul has learned lessons of the road and once you have scrapped the body then its time soon after to get a new one!!!!! The human spirit is the driver and it gets wiser over the years. A man got into my taxi once and we were talking about our bodies. He said that some people had Ferrari bodies. They polished them everyday. Raced them every now and again and serviced them regularly and put the most expensive fuel and oil in them and showed off to people at the side of the road, making them stare... Some people have Fords. Scream them around for a few years at 100 miles an hour, crash a few times but they have had loads of fun. A bit non-descript and had no one looking at them in wonder. But, as with all cars they get scrapped eventually. Just like the human body. I thought this was an excellent way to look at life and the soul. If you're supposed to be very flash and good looking in life then great. But if your non descript or maybe, in some peoples eyes, odd. Then whatever, it's none of anyone else's business. As long as you are enjoying your life and you have people around you that care for you. Then I think that's a life more fulfilled. Most of all, you may not have to come back here again if you live life to its fullest. It's how you get on with life that matters, not how you look externally. As long as you never hurt anyone else in this life and you show love and understanding and are non-judgemental to anyone you will be ok. I believe that we all return over and over until we have learned our lessons. The lessons are different everytime we come here. We may be rich in one life and poor in another. We need to experience everything. One life we may be someone that inflicts pain on people and another we have to know what's it's like, to have that pain inflicted upon ourselves. It's about balance. We have to learn to be more 'God Like' in our lives. It's about learning who we are and what the world is about. It's about embracing spirituality within our selves and giving it back to others. We need to go through so many lives to get it right. Each time we come back here, which happens to be the best place to learn, we erase our external memory. Our soul keeps everything within its own memory. So we then can start over and try to get it right. We have told our guides of our plans and they then help us along the road to getting it right this time. Every now and again someone will have a memory of a past life. I think this is for a reason. We sometimes need to remember what we did before to rectify what we are doing this time. That's why some people have past life regression and it helps them come to terms with why they feel certain things in this lifetime.

Reincarnation has been scientifically proved beyond reasonable doubt by the amazing works of Professor Ian Stevenson of the University of Virginia.

He has gone through several thousand case studies and proved it. If you get a chance buy the book "The Children who have Lived Before" It's amazing and just goes to prove that we do come back. But again, please believe in what you want and separate what you don't need.

Miscarriage/Abortion?

I HAVE HAD experience of this and it never gets easier to understand why after the joy of finding out you're going to have a baby that the baby dies and you feel lost and have so many questions. Spirit has helped me when my ex wife had a miscarriage, in understanding why this had to happen. A spirit, once the blueprint is sorted and once it's chosen its new parents, it then sometimes jumps in and out of the body growing inside to check in on its progress. Sometimes the body may have problems and it decides that it's not the right body to jump into or the circumstances in the parent's life it's not the right time. I also think that in abortion the mother has no say in what happens. It's all meant to be and the spirit influences how the outcome of the pregnancy is going to unfold. It's not the mothers fault. It's whatever they and the new spirit have to learn in this lifetime. I believe that the spirit then decides whether to come along later, as with most people, you find that they have had a miscarriage and then had a full term pregnancy. The spirit may decide that it's going to be born to a close member of the family. It can still then take part in that person's life but in a different way, a different angle. I believe that a the spirit literally arrives in the body of a baby the moment of birth... It's the reason why some babies cry when they are born. The spirit has been shocked into the body and is thinking "Oh no, not this again" But also that's why some babies don't cry and just look around them. They are seasoned pros at life and have decided to come back for maybe one last time and they look at you as if to say "come on then, let's get on with it" How many times have you heard someone say "That baby has been here before"? They have.

My child has an imaginary friend?

MOST CHILDREN WHO have imaginary friends are actually in contact with spirit. These imaginary friends are not as made up as parents want to believe. Children are new from spirit. They are closer to it than us and are acutely more aware. They don't know not to question that a spirit may be in their company and talking to them, because to them this is perfectly natural. You should talk to your children about their friends. Ask them who they are talking to and ask questions about them. I think you will be very surprised. But as with grandparents, you need to spend more time trying to understand by asking questions. If you ask you're four year old for instance "what was it like before you were born" then you may be surprised to hear from them a detailed account of what it was like in spirit? I remember holding a newborn once and looking into his eyes and seeing in my head how long he planned before he came here. And got and answer straight away. 14 months. It freaked me out a bit to hear this voice in my head coming from his spirit. It was amazing. There are a few books you can buy on this subject. Be more open to what your children are saying it's an amazing experience.

What is Déjà vu?

THERE ARE MANY forms of this. I think sometimes we catch up on ourselves. Hence someone will say something to you and its snaps in your mind that you have heard them say that before in the same context at that exact time. It has to do with your spirit having gone on ahead while you sleep to see that your life is going in the direction that you have set it. So it can move you in that direction when you awaken. That's why some dreams come true. Because your dreams are a product of what has happened that day, or a few days past and also can sometimes predict what's going to happen. The spirit goes forward and checks out what is going on in your near future and then comes back with the information which then becomes a memory to you. It's also like when you go somewhere and you swear that you have been there before. You probably have in different lifetime.

What happens to a child when he or she passes?

WHEN A CHILD passes it goes straight to an area in heaven where it is looked after by family that have passed before or wiser spirits or spirit nannies that take care of him/her. Also a child will grow up in heaven and will go to school and learn more about life than we could ever learn here. Its because of the innocence of a child it will feel no pain when its passes and will be helped every step of the way. They also have no personal judgement.

My dog/cat has died, does it go to heaven?

WHEN A DOG or cat passes away its spirit will stay wherever it was most happy. Normally it will stay with its master and live around you as this is its personal heaven. As I have said in an earlier chapter, my dogs came to see me in a dream and they were running around in the woods playing. Losing a pet is one of the hardest things that anyone has to go through. But as with all spirit, whether animal or human, you choose the people you want to be with and then stay with them after they have passed because that's where they were at their happiest. Also, that's why cats and dogs sometimes inexplicably seem to have a fit and do strange things around you like running around or barking at nothing you can see... They can feel the presence of the other animal.

Where do we go?

I THINK IT'S different for everyone. Every person has his or her personal heaven once you have passed through one level of consciousness. This level is the one that you go to when we have just passed over. We are met by our friends and family that have passed on before us. We are then shown our own movie, a kind of story of our life. We then find out what we have learned from that incarnation and decide where and what we are going to do next. We then go to a higher level which is our own personal heaven. We can select where we want to live, who we want to live with and build our own space. We can also go to places that have been built for us. Like schools and libraries. There are also concert halls. Whatever you enjoyed doing on earth you can do in heaven. But, most of the things we enjoy here are physical i.e., smoking, drinking and gambling. After a while we lose these vices and do what we have always enjoyed doing. Our souls are made of love and the best kind of love is spending time with our families and friends. We then after a while, decide whether we are going to come back to learn. So we can either stay behind or choose someone to guide. Or we can help others to cross over when they pass. We can also decide whether we want to come back and learn. Sometimes it takes years to come back. Or rather it seems to take years to us. But time and space is different upstairs. It doesn't exist. So what may feel like hundreds of years to us it could feel like two years to them.

What are Soul Mates and will I ever meet mine?

SOUL MATES ARE spirit that has decided to walk and learn throughout different lifetimes with you. A soul mate can be anyone, not only a partner but a close friend, family member or even a beloved pet. Most times it works out that soul mates will be a partner. What people don't understand is that a soul mate may not be a relationship that works out in this lifetime. I know from experience that my soul mate has travelled through many lifetimes with me and has caused me personal pain in some lives and total love in others. But I have understood that the reason she does this is because I have decided with the blueprint that I have to learn how to love and loose and also learn how to get myself up off the floor, brush myself off and start all over again. So, it's not going to necessarily mean that we meet our soul mate and spend the rest of our life in sheer bliss. You may have already met your mate but it didn't workout. So please don't hold on for someone who seems perfect in every way. Just let life happen and if we are to meet that special person then just let time take its course. Our spirit guides will point us in the right direction at the time.

What happens to bad people?

THEY GO TO the same place. We take our thoughts, feelings and personality with us. So if we were a nasty piece of work in this life we have a lot further to go and a lot more to learn. There is a kind of judgment. The spirit is aware that it's had hurt many people in its lifetime and that its does have a lot to answer for. A spirit has to be given a chance to explain itself and make amends. They also have one of two options open to them. They can come back straight away to repay their Karmic debt. Or they may become a sort of guide to help people who have caused pain here realise their errors.

Can you switch your ability on and off?

IT'S SOMETHING THAT you have to learn over the years. It's a strange experience when a spirit comes through. It starts off when it's time to get to work. If you are doing a reading for someone either at a house or in front of an audience, you first need to relax sometime during the day. As I have said in other chapters. This can be done however it works for you.

I normally get into my car and take the dog for a walk to the woods. While in my car I like to listen to some CDs I have made up. Which have songs from my favourite bands REM and Sigur Ros. When it's closer to the time that I have to work, I like to have a few minutes to myself where I speak to my brother and guides in spirit and ask that I don't let them down and also that I can get a message to people that really need it in the audience. After the evening is over I then take a bit of time to talk to people and get their reaction both negative and positive. Then I wind down and relax by either driving home with some comedy Cds or get home, thank spirit and then watch some TV to take my mind off what has happened and shut down. It's different for all of us but this works for me.

What does it feel like when you get a spirit through?

IT FEELS LIKE you are being wrapped up in cotton wool. After a while you start to lose your breath and sometimes it feels like when you are just about to cry over a sad movie you have to try and stop yourself and try to catch your breath. Then afterwards you feel like that old saying that someone has walked over your grave. You feel sort of light headed and then nothing. The communication stops and you know its time to get to the next one. It's quite a wonderful feeling. But it is different for everyone. This is just how I feel when I get a strong connection through. You may feel different sensations. But there is no denying the fact that it's amazing.

Is it great to be a medium?

IT'S THE MOST amazing thing in the world but it also sucks sometimes. When you get a connection through for someone and they go away feeling lighter and understanding a little more of what has happened to a loved one, it's an amazing feeling for both of you. It can sometimes be a bit of an ego trip. But don't let your ego take over as spirit have this amazing way of shutting down if your heads getting too big and then they make you feel like a twat a few times to bring you back down to earth. Other times it's a very lonely life. Most people just want the message. They don't care if it's you or a monkey in a top hat giving the message over. At first you are open all the time. You want to read for anyone that bumps into you in the street or anyone in the pub. That goes on for a while. But it's not a good idea to be open all the time. Otherwise you might as well stay at work 24/7. You need your own space and relax time. And once you realise this, spirit then gives you a break from connecting and you start to enjoy being you and not a Medium.

Do you believe in GOD?

YES. I COULDN'T do this work without a belief in god. I don't believe that God is a man in the Monty Python sense. You know giant hands and a big booming voice from heaven. But I believe in an energy force that holds everything together, energy of love. I don't think that God is there to be worshipped and to spend your life worried about carrying favour with the almighty and stuff. I think we are here to learn to be more god-like. Like I have said a hundred times, you believe in what you want to believe. But there are some people who go out of their way to worry you about God. I pray, but to the energy of God. I ask for help for people all over. I'm not going to sit there worrying about whether I should be asking god for forgiveness. I don't believe that it's like that. I think we all should know that what we do sometimes is wrong. Spirit kicks your arse anyway when you do something to someone that you shouldn't.

What if I go to see a medium and get nothing through?

THIS HAPPENS MORE times than you will get something. Spirit will come to you when they are ready to make the connection and with which medium they want to use. If you got to see a medium as part of a group, think of it like a wedding. The wedding is for two people and the couple in question have their names on all the invitations. It's also their choice where they hold the wedding. It's their day. But you are all invited to share their day and you go away from that with a feeing like either you are remembering your own wedding. Or what your wedding would feel like. Plus you get a piece of cake to take with you too. So everyone gets a connection when you go to see a medium. Not just the ones that the medium talks too.

What is a Ghost?

A GHOST AND a spirit are two totally separate things. A ghost is an imprint on time and is a dead energy. Whereas a spirit is still alive, just living in a different way. A ghost is an energy of something that happened in the past. When people see or feel ghosts what they are seeing and feeling is a negative energy force that due to certain conditions within an area manifests itself into an almost video re run. What you are seeing or feeling usually, is something that happened in the past. The spirits of these people have long gone to heaven or been re incarnated. When someone dies tragically their imprint is left behind in that area. If there has been multiple passing due to an accident or major event, the energy that those people felt stays within the walls of the building or the area that they passed in. I have heard many ghost stories that have told of grey ladies and shrieking women or moaning men walking past. Some have been seen to walk on a different level than the floor that exists at that time

I heard a story once about a school in Oxford. My friend Tony went there. There was a story about a boy that had committed suicide through bullying around 50 years ago. He had thrown himself off the top flight of stairs and had hit one of the banisters on the way down. Once a year, on the anniversary of his passing, there would be a dent in the new replaced banisters for a few minutes. It would also appear to be cracked with wood splinters. But then it would go back to being an untouched banister again.

I have been asked lots of times to come to people's houses and tell them whether they are haunted and who they are haunted by. Well, I have been able to pick up on the energies in these houses. But I am medium that is able to connect with living spirits and mostly unable to connect with dead energy. Although I do pick up on negative energy because I am sensitive, as a medium, to most forms of energy.

Why can't I connect with spirits but can tell the future accurately?

I THINK IT'S because we are all different in our abilities and what we have been chosen to do with this gift. As I have said in this book I started out doing Tarot card readings for friends. I was pretty accurate with them but as time went on I found myself being interrupted more by spirit. So I was told by upstairs that I should be connecting people instead. I'm not saying anything's wrong with doing cards and telling people what they can expect. It's all from spirit anyway; cards are just a focal point. That's why some people read playing cards or tea leaves. It's not about what the cards are telling them. It's about what spirit are saying through whatever medium that's been chosen. Some people won't go and see a medium. They don't want to find out about who has passed over. They want to know what's going to happen to them in the future. I think if you're meant to help people out that way then that is what you have been given this ability to do. Some tarot readers are amazing. We have all been given different ways of helping people. You could end up being a psychic healer using Reiki healing or you could do regression therapy or even counselling. They are all part of being in contact with spirit. The main thing about all these abilities is that you're helping people. So if you find your wondering why you can't do amazing card readings or you may not be able to heal people. It's because you may have to try all these things out until spirit guides help you find what you are supposed to do. It doesn't make you crap because you can tell the future and not heal. Or you can connect people and not tell the future. It's from spirit.

What is Karma?

KARMA IS THE universal debt system. Not like these commercials that offer to consolidate loans etc into one easily affordable payment. Everyone has heard the saying "You reap what you sow" Well, you have to go through many lifetimes to get your spirit cleansed and pure and to become more God-like. We all make mistakes during our lifetimes. We are supposed to learn from them, but sometimes free will rakes over. It's a natural thing but our free will can be used to help or hinder others. As we travel through each lifetime on our journey we have to payback whatever bad Karma our free will has accumulated over the time we are here. If you were mean in one lifetime to a particular person then you may have to experience this happening to yourself in another lifetime. In some lifetimes if we were really good people and did nothing but help others. We will get that back. Karma can also be good as well as bad. We repay our debts. The otherside of this coin is that we can pay back Karma from this lifetime in this lifetime. We don't have to pass over and be reborn. We can be reborn every second of everyday. We just have to want it and do something about it ourselves. We have all heard people say that so and so has turned over a new leaf. Maybe they were criminals or drug dealers etc. They spent time in prison and became a new person. Well, it's exactly the same for everyone. The other saying is

"I must have done something pretty bad in a previous life to deserve what I have to put up with now" That's right you probably did. But it's up to you to sort it out.

I'm not a medium, how do I know spirits are around?

THERE ARE SOME ways that spirit will show themselves to you. These are often around the house. As spirit is energy and not physical anymore, they are able to influence certain things around the house. Sometimes they will turn the TV on and off. Or maybe change the channel on your remote control or start up the stereo. They may also flicker the lights or turn the kettle on etc. They are able to do this easily as they are energy and the appliances I have talked about use electricity. If something like this occurs in the house. Then ask who it is and ask them to repeat the process. Remember it will always be the first person that you think of. Don't analyze the situation, just go with it. I have also found that when spirits appear in the house they may well move something. This maybe your keys or a letter or something personal like your watch. It's amazing as you know you left it in a certain place. As you hunt around the house, you go back to the place you think you left it originally and there it is! Still there! It's just that spirit have moved it to get your attention. I suggest that before you try to find it, ask for it back. You may feel silly talking to thin air. But ask the spirits for your item back. By acknowledging the spirit has hidden the item they should return it to you.

An example of this was my mother came back from America just before Christmas. She had bought a hefty Christmas tree ornament. It was shaped like a fireplace. You had to put a fairy light in it and it looked like a fire in the grate. I liked it but my mum LOVED it. She is always getting decorations and lights from the USA. She insists they are bigger and better. I'm not much of a Christmas fan so I just thought I would humour her. One morning she called me on the phone. She was a little distraught. She told me her decoration had gone missing from her tree. I then told her I would come over for a cuppa and we will see if we can find it. She looked everywhere under the tree and in the branches. I said she was wasting her time looking under the tree as it was huge and you couldn't miss it. I then suggested that we ask spirit for it back. I asked who may have it and my uncle Roger who had passed the Christmas before came into my head. It was his way of showing himself to my mum. She had also been very upset around the anniversary of his passing. I then told my mum to acknowledge him and ask for it back. We went into the kitchen for a cuppa. When we entered the room ten minutes later, it was there where it had been all along. - On the Christmas tree.

My mum has since had lots of things go missing and things moved around the house. It doesn't scare her anymore. She knows its spirits way of getting through. She sometimes sits and demands her stuff back. It's quite funny to hear her telling upstairs off for hiding her stuff. But I try not to embarrass her when I hear her.

Can people be possessed by bad spirits?

NO. YOU HAVE seen movies like The Entity or Poltergeist Two, where the main characters have been taken over by so called evil spirits. They have not been taken over at all by evil spirits. Evil spirits don't exist. We have all been to heaven so many times through millennia that when we get to there we are cleansed. We have learned through our life review what we did in this lifetime. Then we are taken off to learn and for some to be healed from our ways in our last incarnation. Obviously there are lots of nasty people in this world. We do need some negative to balance out the positive. If everyone on this existence were positive, loving, god like souls it would be an amazing place to live. But we wouldn't learn anything. So we may as well have stayed in heaven.

I believe that possession is good vs. bad energy within the environment. Some people, like mediums, are over sensitive to positive and negative energy. If you are in a concert and having a great time, you feel everyone else's positive energy and that helps you to have a good time and makes you feel on a real high. If you were to go to a funeral, you feel really sad, even if you didn't really know the person. You are picking up on everyone else's negative energy.

As a medium, your sensitivity is heightened. You need a heightened sensitivity to do this work as you are connecting with energy. You're not talking to a person; you are talking to energy, using your spirit which is pure energy to reach their spirit, which is pure energy. Possession is tonnes of negative energy within an environment which is felt one hundred fold, by an over sensitive person.

If I go to a certain area in my hometown which has such a high amount of poverty, drug and alcohol abuse and broken families, I feel really bad. It makes me feel so repressed and I get a real down feeling for the time I'm there. If you live in an environment where say, a person was murdered or physically or mentally abused, then the energy tends to stay there and not move on. It will stay even stronger if there is negativity with the current residents. If one of those people is hypersensitive to it, then they may be taken over by the negativity. If the new owners of the house have loads of positive energy, this may slightly counteract the negative. Although it's kind of like putting chocolate chips onto a cowpat. Hence, some people seem possessed. But they are just over sensitive to a negative energy area.

As you become more aware of your ability, you will need to ask your spirit guides to put protection into place. They will normally have done this already. But it's not like some people say, to protect you from evil spirits. Like I said, they do not exist. It's to protect your over sensitive energy from receiving negativity. I have my bouncers as I like to call them. Two doormen who watch out for me. Your names not down so you aint coming in. They stop the negativity from getting to me while I work. Negativity from the environment, it's hard sometimes when getting a connection, not to blub your eyes out, but you are protected from it. You need to almost grow a thick skin. But one that doesn't make you seem like you don't care, it's just the opposite. You do care, a lot, about getting the message across. We do this for love and because we can. But, if it means you go around getting stung by negativity all the time, it would mess with your head too much.

Does a psychic ability come from family?

WE ARE ALL psychic so I'm not sure that family genes have anything to do with it. I do however think that having psychics in the family helps. Mainly because if being psychic has been accepted within a family, then your own abilities will be accepted more and also may be encouraged to grow. It's the same with re-incarnation. Many western beliefs don't cater for re-incarnation. So if a child talks about a previous life he or she is told off for talking rubbish. Yet many beliefs in Asia encourage families to listen out for the children telling about past lives. So I believe that if you suspect any child of being psychic then please encourage them to tell you how they feel. If you encourage their ability then they won't shy away from it in the future.

I heard not so long ago about my dads father Thomas. I had no idea that he was psychic until a couple of years ago. We were all sitting in The Winchester Arms in Portsmouth having a few drinks. My father had come from Wales for a couple of days. My uncle mark was there and my friend Mark. We all had a great laugh together going over embarrassing stories about what Mark and I used to get up to as teenagers together.

Towards the end of the evening the conversation got round to what I do. My Uncle Mark said that he was very sceptical on the subject. In his words it was a load of old tosh!! To my surprise, my dad pointed out that I got the ability from his father.

I couldn't believe it.

As the story goes he used to do tea leaf readings and palmistry in the nineteen fifties. He would do it just before a shift for workers at a dairy in Whitland,

Carmarthenshire, where he worked. He was very good at what he did. My dad said his predictions always came true.

I can assume this to be true.

It reminded me of something that happened about 10 years before. My first wife was in St Mary's Hospital, Portsmouth having our first child. It was a particularly bad birth. The doctors said that she might not make it as she was losing oxygen. They had to deliver via Von tous, a big plug that sits on the head of the baby and sucks on. Then with a chain at the other end they then pull like mad to get the baby out. It was touch and go for a while but she was born ok and in good health. That night I was sitting in the hospital, dozing off with my wife and daughter, when I noticed a shadow walk past the curtain. I thought it might be a doctor or nurse doing a round, when suddenly a short little man with glasses, a hat and a brown suit poked his head round the curtain. I said hello, and asked what he wanted. He said not to be alarmed but he was just checking in on the baby. I showed him my daughter. My wife was asleep so we talked in whispers. He said that she was very beautiful and she would grow to be an amazing child. I thanked him and he left. I thought I recognized him, but couldn't place his face. Afterwards I asked the nurse whether she knew the man who came around late that evening. She said that visiting hours were over then and there were no other fathers on the ward. I didn't know what to think but I was sure that they had made a mistake. Who could he have been? It kind of freaked me out to think that these people were walking the maternity wards at night when they weren't allowed and I had showed him my new daughter. But I still didn't see any malice in him. I thought of him as a kind old man that liked to see the new born. I still felt though that I knew him.

While we were visiting my father in Wales I asked him to show me a photograph of his father. I had never seen him before as he had passed before I was born. And it came as a shock when it turned out to be the same man who turned up at the bedside that night in hospital.

ABOUT THIS SECTION:

None of us will ever totally understand what happens until we pass away ourselves. I think we suddenly get a greater understanding of how life works and why there are some amazing people that come into our lives and some really nasty ones too. And also why some of the most wonderful things and some horrific things happen to us. I think we are all taught all the answers when we get to the other side. I have spirit to thank for the answers in this chapter. They have given me an insight into what goes on. But I have only just broken the surface. One day I will understand what happens fully. But in the meantime I hope that the questions and answers section of this book has helped you to get a bit more of an understanding of how this all comes about. Why we are here and for what reason we have to go through this life.

I can give you the answers because.......

I AM A MEDIUM

Chapter Thirty

FROM A TO B

AT THE TIME of writing this book I am still arranging new venues to do my mediumship demonstrations, doing readings at home. Also readings on the telephone to people who can't get to see me personally. I am also still giving spiritual guidance and help via e-mail.

My main hope for the future is that this book will reach a great many people.

Throughout this whole arduous, interesting, painful and sometimes laughable process of getting to where I am today, I have strived to keep all of this "real" as they say.

I'm not a well known medium. I don't have a television show of my own or fill massive three thousand seat theatres when I come to town. But I know that I am helping lots of people through the work I have done and my work in the future.

Some mediums do become very well known through their work, others don't ever wish to be well known and soldier on quietly. There are thousands that work regular jobs and tour the church circuit week in, week out. I don't suppose I will ever be filling Wembley Stadium, not that I would want to. I have come to a point where I feel that it doesn't matter how many people come and see me, as long as I can help at least one person, to deal with a loss in their own life. I believe that the others still go away with the sense of connection to their friends and family that have crossed over. I am very happy with the way I have finally taken on board the full extent to which my ability heals.

We, as humans, are very complex. The body is just a vehicle for carrying the soul - to learn lessons here on this tiny speck of a planet, lost in the infinite whirls of space. When the body dies, our eternal spirit lives on in a very different way. Everyone has the ability to connect as we are all spirit. There are still those who say that Psychic Medium's are modern day charlatans, preying on people's weaknesses and yearnings. I haven't made much money out of this. I am not and never will be a rich man, financially. But I feel very rich spiritually. I know that I have helped people through just being me. No frills, no expectations. Just an average Joe that has maybe an above average ability. I love my job and so you may take it or leave it. If it works for you then "go for it." Never be told who or what you are and always take advice from everyone and use the bits that are helpful to you and nothing more.

Everyone is special, regardless of your religion, colour or sexual orientation. If you are a nice person and have lots of friends, then you will go a long way in this lifetime. Damn anyone that puts you down or tries to stop you living your dream. My dream is to make that connection for thousands of people. I admit that it gives me a lot of satisfaction when I get told that I was "spot on". It really helps and strengthens my own beliefs in my ability. This isn't some mind reading trick as some people would have you believe. I'm not that clever for a start!

We all have the same connection. Mediums are not gods, they are not something special. It's not a gift exclusive to certain people. It's an ability that we all share. We are one of the same. We are all human spirit. People come up to me and thank me for the connection and often say wow you are so amazing at what you do. And I explain to them that they need to thank the spirit world, not me. I am just a small part in this amazing process.

I was chosen to do this with my life. At first not out of choice. I have certainly been through some ups and downs to get here. But as the years go by, I am enjoying it more and more. It's an amazing feeling every time I connect for someone and they go away knowing they have been reached by loved ones and received messages from the other side for whatever purpose. This job is the most wonderful job in the world. I feel lucky and blessed that spirit is coming through to me to talk to these people.

Thanks for finding this book. I really appreciate all of you. With this work I hope to have touched a few hearts and made a few peoples lives a little easier to live. I believe I have done what I have set out to do. That is to have a greater knowledge of the spirit world and my own spirituality as I hope you have through this work.

Be happy in this lifetime and don't take any rubbish from anyone. Most of all, keep an open mind. We are all capable of doing this. We are all born of the same thing, spirit. Give a little of yourself everyday and you will get back so much more.

I AM JUST ME.

I AM A MEDIUM.

I WOULD LIKE to thank the people listed here individually and collectively for all their support.

Mark Evans. Mum and joe, Michelle and Brent, DAD and WSM. My Daughters... Sue. Steve Dartnell. Nadine, Susie, Dawn, Lisa. Uncle Mark. Auntie Liz, Ruth and Becky, Bob Pitman, Phil Carpenter, Lindsay Lou. Chris Childs. Sonya, Juliette, Colin, Kelly. Vixter. Karen and the twins. Justin Mason. Carol and Lynn. Claire and Jess, Mark. Richie Williams. Steve and Michelle. All my friends out there on the Taxi Ranks of Portsmouth... Marcie. Tina, Amy Jo. Dana, Kieran and Ruth. Gitch, Phil, Helena, Odd Job, John, Darren, Shaun Theresa ,Julia. My Family and friends

I would like to thank all those people that allowed me to use their experiences in this book. Also to people I haven't named here. You are special to me and thanks for everything we have been through.

And also thanks to all my friends and people who have come to see me and I have met along the way. You're all special to me in your own unique way. Thanks so much for trusting me to make the connections I have. You know who you all are. I couldn't have done it without you.

Last but not least a special thank you to spirit. Upstairs has helped me through my life and God willing through the rest of it. I can honestly say that I trust in you fully and I want to thank you for waiting and trusting in me.

Love to you all.

If you have any comments or questions on this book and your own spiritual pathway then please e-mail me direct.

spiritualgateways@hotmail.com

I answer all e-mails personally.

I hope to hear from you all soon.

Printed in Great Britain
by Amazon